FEEL HAPPY NOW!

Also by Michael Neill

YOU CAN HAVE WHAT YOU WANT:
Proven Strategies for Inner and Outer Success

Hay House Titles of Related Interest

ASK AND IT IS GIVEN: *Learning to Manifest Your Desires,*
by Esther and Jerry Hicks (The Teachings of Abraham™)

AN ATTITUDE OF GRATITUDE: *21 Life Lessons,*
by Keith D. Harrell

COUNT YOUR BLESSINGS:
The Healing Power of Gratitude and Love,
by Dr. John F. Demartini

EVERYDAY POSITIVE THINKING,
by Louise L. Hay and Friends

EVERYTHING YOU NEED TO KNOW TO FEEL GO(O)D,
by Candace B. Pert, Ph.D., with Nancy Marriott

FOUR ACTS OF PERSONAL POWER: *How to Heal Your Past
and Create a Positive Future,* by Denise Linn

GRATITUDE: *A Way of Life,* by Louise L. Hay and Friends

THE POWER OF INTENTION: *Learning to Co-create Your World
Your Way,* by Dr. Wayne W. Dyer

YOUR DESTINY SWITCH: *Master Your Key Emotions, and
Attract the Life of Your Dreams!* by Peggy McColl

All of the above are available at your local bookstore,
or may be ordered by visiting:

Hay House USA: **www.hayhouse.com**®
Hay House Australia: **www.hayhouse.com.au**
Hay House UK: **www.hayhouse.co.uk**
Hay House South Africa: **www.hayhouse.co.za**
Hay House India: **www.hayhouse.co.in**

FEEL HAPPY NOW!

Michael Neill

HAY HOUSE, INC.
Carlsbad, California • New York City
London • Sydney • Johannesburg
Vancouver • Hong Kong • New Delhi

Published and distributed in the United States by: Hay House, Inc.: www.
hayhouse.com • **Published and distributed in Australia by:** Hay House
Australia Pty. Ltd.: www.hayhouse.com.au • **Published and distributed
in the United Kingdom by:** Hay House UK, Ltd.: www.hayhouse.co.uk •
Published and distributed in the Republic of South Africa by: Hay House
SA (Pty), Ltd.: www.hayhouse.co.za • **Distributed in Canada by:** Raincoast:
www.raincoast.com • **Published in India by:** Hay House Publishers India:
www.hayhouse.co.in

Editorial supervision: Jill Kramer • *Design:* Riann Bender

Every effort has been made to obtain necessary permission with reference to copyright
material. The publishers apologize if inadvertently any sources remain unacknowledged and
will be glad to make the necessary arrangements at the earliest opportunity.

Dr. Richard Bandler's techniques used with written permission. Visit **www.richardbandler.com**
to learn more.

The Sacred Journey technique used with the written permission of Robert Dilts. Please see
"Tools of the Spirit" and the "Encyclopedia of Systemic NLP" for more information.

Library of Congress Cataloging-in-Publication Data

Neill, Michael.
  Feel happy now! / Michael Neill. -- 1st ed.
    p. cm.
  ISBN-13: 978-1-4019-1773-9 (tradepaper) 1. Happiness. I. Title.
  BF575.H27N45 2008
  152.4'2--dc22   2007014300

ISBN: 978-1-4019-1773-9

11 10 09 08   4 3 2 1
1st edition, January 2008

Printed in the United States of America

*To Mom and Dad and Charlie and Dale
for believing in me when nobody else would . . .
and to Michael, aged 13 to 20*

"This is the true joy in life, the being used for a purpose recognized by yourself as a mighty one; the being thoroughly worn out before you are thrown on the scrap heap; the being a force of Nature instead of a feverish selfish little clod of ailments and grievances complaining that the world will not devote itself to making you happy."

— George Bernard Shaw

CONTENTS

FOREWORD

by **Candace B. Pert**, Ph.D.,
the author of *Everything You Need to Know to Feel Go(o)d*

We're all familiar with the phenomenon of the formidable chore. It may be a closet that needs cleaning or a garage that needs emptying out. We resist it like crazy, building up a mountain of reasons why now is *not* the time, and our lives are too full or busy to take on even one more task.

Then one day, in one moment, we feel different—and within five minutes, the whole job is done. It's not just about how much sugar is flowing through our muscles at any given time that determines our level of activity and interactivity with life. Our consciousness has a power and rhythm of its own.

The human mind can propel the body through a chore (like organizing a closet) when it's in the right mood; and while no one would say that cleaning out a closet is a purely psychological act, the biggest hurdle to getting things done isn't in our bodies but in our psyche. It's with the mind that we turn the flow of energy on or off in the body. Yet somehow in our culture today, drugging the brain to alter its chemistry has become unrealistically overemphasized in terms of the role it plays in controlling our moods.

My background, education, and work is as a research scientist. For the past 20 years, I've been developing an AIDS drug that's leading to an effective vaccine for the HIV virus, but I was originally trained in a neuropharmacology laboratory. We pioneered the development of specific receptor-active drugs that increased serotonin and went on to become a new class of highly touted antidepressants. I was there to watch rapid progress in neuroscience lead to the destigmatization of mental illness—a good thing by any stretch of the imagination.

Yet believe it or not, the popular idea of a "chemical imbalance" hasn't been rigorously proven scientifically! Yes, blaming depression on a shortage of serotonin makes a lovely sound bite for television commercials and pharmaceutical brochures, but the conclusive evidence that antidepressants work through this mechanism isn't actually there. True, important drugs that reverse clinical depression do block the uptake of serotonin into rat brain nerve endings in test tubes; however, to cite one fly in the ointment, this uptake inhibition happens immediately, while the depression itself doesn't lift for three weeks.

Based on recent data implicating lipid metabolism in so-called bipolar disorder (a moving-target diagnosis that's been changed three times in my professional lifetime), I suspect that at its root, mental illness is about the rhythm of energy flow throughout the entire body—not in a "cosmic," mysterious sense, but in the amount of actual energy available for our brains and bodies to use.

The idea that we can magically fix a chemical imbalance in the brain with drugs also remains scientifically unproven, and the gross overprescribing of psychoactive drugs is potentially dangerous. As the data has shown, a small percentage of both young people and adults has had severe violent reactions toward themselves and others in response to the proliferation of this kind of medication as a "cure-all" for life's most fundamental problems.

Taking drugs has replaced working on yourself and your life—and now that anti-anxiety and antidepressant medications can be prescribed by any type of physician, the lack of counseling and sensitivity to the power of consciousness as a healing force has become endemic.

In sharp contrast to this approach, Michael Neill steps forward in this book as a powerful spokesman for the wonderful world of the mind. He offers clear, practical ways to manage your moods effectively without drugs. These techniques go beyond the traditional offerings of psychotherapy or even cognitive-behavioral therapy and get into the heart of what's possible. There's no mind-body split—there's always something you can do to make things better.

This book also offers a "happy" alternative to the victim mentality of conventional medical treatment. Through stories of his own battles with depression and the work he has done with clients over the past 16 years, Michael paints a vivid picture of how much of what we feel is actually under our own direct control.

His experience in the realms of thought management through the application of Neuro-Linguistic Programming (NLP) and other cognitive and somatic disciplines is extensive, yet his explanations of how to use these tools to manage our moods quickly and easily are a joy to read and practice. Simply put, we can all learn to make ourselves happy, and this book will show you exactly how to do it.

One caveat: Clinical depression is a very serious and potentially fatal disease, and neither Michael nor I would argue that you can just will away violent or suicidal tendencies. Antidepressants can be helpful even though we don't really know how they work yet, but it's been proven that they're most effective when given in addition to therapeutic counseling.

While the techniques in this book are potentially useful even in clinical situations, they'll work best in conjunction with a holistic and inclusive approach. Our brains run on sugar (glucose) in a narrow zone of regulation; therefore, how much of it we consume has a profound effect on our moods.

At the end of the day, getting to know yourself and how your emotions are impacted by the foods you eat and the amount of sleep and exercise you get will form an important part of your personal program for happiness.

Perhaps I can sum it up best by sharing the story of a young friend of mine whose mother suffered from a diagnosis of bipolar disorder for many years. His whole life has been affected by this and the widespread belief that he's "doomed" to inherit unhappiness through his genetic makeup. In fact, there's no clear scientific evidence proving that either depression or anxiety is a genetically transmitted disease.

Yes, stress, anxiety, and depression (and for that matter, life itself!) can be extremely difficult to deal with, but the real burden is believing there's nothing we can do about it.

Let's face it—all of us are moody. We may hide our emotions in the dark closets of our mind, forcing ourselves each morning to go to jobs that we don't enjoy and smile at colleagues we don't really know (and who don't really know us). We may even resist the "chore" of cleaning up our thinking . . . and our lives.

And this ultimately leads us to the promise of this practical and important book: When we learn to manage our thoughts and bring love to the front of our mind, that love can override and even transform the "brain chemistry" fueling our bodies, actions, and lives.

Our culture has swung so far to the "pill for every ill" extreme that I think it's vital for everyone to be exposed to the unique and fresh perspective you're about to discover. Regardless of any academic debate it may cause, I'm going to recommend this book to my young friend. It's clear to me that what Michael Neill has to say works. Read this book and feel happy!

Preface

MY STORY

A very learned philosopher dreamed that God appeared to him and offered him the choice between complete knowledge and complete happiness. Being a scholarly man, he chose complete knowledge. When asked to review what he had learned, he said he realized one thing: He had made the wrong choice.

From the age of 13 until I was around 20, I alternated between depression and mania, barely able to get out of bed on some days and unable to get back into it on others. My attempts to self-medicate with alcohol, tobacco, and other less-legal substances never seemed to work for more than a few hours; and as the various cocktails I mixed inside my body became more elaborate, the feelings (and my ability to deal with them) grew more severe.

One particularly bad night when I was in college, I remember collapsing into fits of uncontrollable sobbing in my dorm room. While this wasn't as unusual an occurrence as I would have liked, this time it was considerably worse—when it hadn't stopped by 1 A.M., I recognized that I needed help. I managed to drag myself down to the campus infirmary, push the night-call button, and collapse in a heap by the door.

After what seemed like hours but was probably only a few minutes, a night nurse came to the door. She took one look at me and—no doubt ignoring years of training and university protocol—cradled me in her arms and began reciting the Lord's Prayer.

She kept encouraging me to join in, and as I didn't have the energy to explain that I only knew the words because I'd recently played Peter in a deaf-theater production of *Jesus Christ Superstar,* I joined in for all I was worth, choking out each line between huge rolling waves of sobbing.

After a few minutes of rocking and praying, the wailing subsided and I began to feel a sense of peace. Perhaps if I'd been a bit riper for conversion, I might have chalked it up to the power of God and converted to Christianity on the spot, but I was still very green in the ways of religion. Instead, I marveled at this woman's ability to "love me" back to some modicum of sanity.

She then took me to a doctor's office to wait, assuring me that they'd help make me better. The doctor, a fine southern gentleman in his early 50s with thick gray hair and a charming smile, asked me a few questions.

"How long has this been going on?"

"Since I was 13." I paused, then added encouragingly, "But only daily for the past month."

He didn't seem unduly encouraged.

"Come with me."

He led me down a long hallway, up a short flight of stairs, and back down the same hallway on the second floor.

It was late, and we were seemingly the only ones there.

Opening a door with a set of keys he carried around his neck, the doctor led me into a pristine hospital room and encouraged me to lie down on the bed and rest. Exhausted as I was from hours of sobbing, that was a very enticing prospect.

"I'll go get something to help you sleep and make you feel better," he said. "We'll admit you in the morning."

When the door shut behind him, I had a moment of incredible clarity: I was at a turning point, and my life was about to change forever. In a way, the choice I had to make was simple. If I stayed, I could just hand my brain over to the doctors and let them try to sort it out for me; if I left, I was going to have to find a way of dealing with the feelings that had overcome me like waves for many years.

I opened the door and looked out, but my nurse friend was now sitting at a desk at the end of the hallway. She didn't see me, and I didn't have the heart to tell her that I was running away.

I stepped back into the room and walked over to the window. Although I was on the second floor, the area below jutted out onto a sort of portico, a mini-rooftop over the mock-Roman colonnades that were all the rage in institutes of higher learning at the time. Gingerly, I opened the window, stepped out onto the roof, and jumped the ten feet or so down to freedom.

While that incident wasn't the end of my battle with depression, anxiety, and stress, it was the beginning of my search for solutions—solutions that can be used by almost anyone to make an immediate difference to your moods, your outlook, and your life. I've refined these techniques with my students and clients over the past 16 years and tested each one of them in the laboratory of my experience. During that time, I've become happier and happier. Now it's your turn. What you are about to read works.

My fondest hope is that this book serves as a turning point in your own quest for happiness, and that these ideas bring as much comfort to your life as they have to mine and those of the countless others who have preceded you on this path. May they prove a trusty guide in your own pursuit of happiness, success, and well-being.

With love,

INTRODUCTION

"I am, by calling, a dealer in words; and words are, of course,
the most powerful drug used by mankind."
— Rudyard Kipling

This is a book about unreasonable happiness. It's about your ability to feel happy not only when you get a promotion, win the lottery, and fall in love with the man or woman of your dreams but also when you lose your job, can't pay the mortgage, and are surrounded by screaming children.

It's about being able to experience good feelings in your body even when good things aren't happening in your life. It's also about why feeling good when things are bad is one of the fastest ways to make them change for the better.

The purpose of this book is for you to become happier—to feel more of your good feelings and be more comfortable with the bad ones. Over the course of the next few hours (or days, weeks, or however long you take to read the book and try out the experiments), you'll learn that you're far more in control of your own well-being than you ever thought possible. You'll discover how to make small changes in the way you feel, think, and act; and you will come to realize that these small changes can make a big (actually, huge) difference.

That's not to say that if you're angry, stressed out,

anxious, or depressed you can or should just "pull yourself together and get on with it." Life is often difficult, and blaming yourself for feeling bad is like trying to teach a pig to sing—it rarely works and tends to annoy the pig.

But if you want to have more choices about what you feel and when, I'll be sharing the fruits of more than 20 years of exploration into the structure of happiness and how you can use that understanding to feel good, feel better, and even feel happy about whatever is happening in your life right now.

How This All Works

My wife once asked me to explain the difference between a therapist, consultant, and coach. I referred to my trusted dictionary and read that a therapist is someone who:

> . . . treats mental, physical, or psychological disorders by mental, physical, or psychological means.

A consultant, on the other hand, is:

> a person who provides expert advice professionally.

Whereas, the standard definition of a coach is:

> a single-decker vehicle, especially one that is comfortably equipped and used for longer journeys.

(This is nothing compared to the Australian definition of a coach as "a docile cow or bullock used as a decoy to attract wild cattle.")

My own definition of these three "helping professionals" is simpler: A therapist fixes what's broken; a consultant tells you what to do; and a coach, like the aforementioned single-decker vehicle, is comfortably equipped and trained to help you get wherever you want to go.

When my wife went on to ask me which one I was, I thought long and hard before realizing that while I inevitably did a little bit of all those things, the heart of my approach didn't really fit any of them. What I am—and the role I hope to play with you throughout this book—is a *catalyst*.

Catalyst (n)

1. An agent or substance that initiates or accelerates the rate of a reaction without being consumed in the process

2. One that precipitates a process or event, especially without being directly involved in or changed by the consequences

3. Someone or something that causes an important event to happen

Much of my background and psychological training is in a field called Neuro-Linguistic Programming (NLP): the study of how language impacts our neurology and behavior. Since what I want is for you to be truly, deeply happy, in order to initiate and accelerate that process I have written this book using specific (and sometimes unusual) language patterns that will actually trigger chemical changes on the inside of your brain. You may begin to experience good feelings in your body and a greater sense of what's possible in your mind just by reading these words.

There are essentially two ways to read this book (or, indeed, any text that purports to tell you how to live more happily in the world): You can believe the book has all the answers, or you can believe that *you* do.

I believe in you.

During the past 16 years, I've worked with more than 10,000 people from all over the world, helping them to become happier and to live more and more wonderful lives. Some of these individuals are among the wealthiest and most successful in the world, while others are "just plain folk" who simply want more out of life than a daily grind and a nightly battle with their own dark thoughts and unfulfilled dreams.

The reason why I can work as effectively with a TV star, CEO, scientist, and housewife all in the same day is that I know something about each one of them that's also true of you:

You already have everything you need inside you to feel happy and live a meaningful life—the only question is access!

I've deliberately put more experiments in this book than anyone is likely to complete. That's so you can do the ones that capture your imagination and leave the rest for another time. Each experiment is designed to give you a tangible experience of your incredible capacity to choose and to change.

And if you choose to make this book about you and your happiness, you are about to embark on an adventure that will change your life for good.

The Choice to Feel Happy

No matter how many times I talk about the benefits of feeling happy to individual clients or groups, the initial responses are the same:

> *"How can I feel happy? You clearly know nothing about my life!"*
>
> *"Isn't it bad to feel happy when there's so much suffering in the world?"*
>
> *"I wouldn't want to feel happy all the time."*

While we'll take a closer look at each of these points in our very first chapter together, allow me to take a few moments here to address them en masse:

You are under no obligation to feel happy. Not feeling happy doesn't make you a bad person, and I don't think that you "should" feel happy now or later or even all the time. But what I do want you to know is that it's possible for you to feel happy—and that choice is yours to make at any moment.

The benefits of making that choice are both simple and profound:

1. It feels good. At the risk of beginning by stating the obvious, the body has a natural predisposition toward pleasure (good feelings) and away from pain (bad feelings). This is a biological survival instinct and is governed by the limbic system and brain stem, which are the oldest parts of the brain. Given the choice between a perceived pain and a perceived pleasure, your brain will take you toward the pleasure and away from the pain every single time.

2. It makes you healthier. When "happy chemicals" are released into your body, your muscles relax and all of your neurological and physiological systems return to their natural state. As most diseases can be traced at least partially to "dis-ease" in the body, this return to ease that accompanies happiness is both comforting at the time and healing over the long term. In addition, a focus on care and compassion increases your body's production of IgA, a chemical that has an immediate positive impact on your immune system.

3. It makes you younger. A study by the Institute of HeartMath has shown that the simple act of visualizing someone you love while focusing your attention on your physical heart will increase your body's production of DHEA, an anti-aging hormone. The beneficial effects of that little bit of good feeling will last in your body for up to seven hours! So not only can feeling happy help you heal, it also acts as a sort of "spiritual Botox," making your skin softer, your eyes brighter, and your entire appearance younger.

4. It makes you smarter. If you've ever struggled to solve a problem, you may have had the experience of being distracted from it by the beauty of a sunset, a well-timed piece of gallows humor, or even the sheer relief of giving up for a period. In the space that followed that interruption, you suddenly knew exactly what to do next.

This process is wonderfully described in Guy Claxton's book *Hare Brain, Tortoise Mind* as "the triumph of wisdom over intellect." Being able to access your inner wisdom "on demand" will make you smarter than another 14 years of school ever could. (As a point of interest, it will also let you take full advantage of everything you learned in the first 14 years.)

5. It makes you more successful. Much of my first book was based on a simple premise:

> *Happiness leads to success a lot more*
> *often than success leads to happiness.*

The clarity of thought and easy flow of inspiration and intuition that accompany good feelings in your body make it easier for you to make the choices that lead to success. They also make success fun.

So in all these ways and more, it turns out that happiness isn't only a choice, it's an extremely practical choice—one that will not only make your life more pleasant, but will make it tangibly better, creating an optimal environment within which you can grow and prosper.

Happy Matters

A venture capitalist I know who's had a great deal of success in his life is what I would call an "open-minded sceptic" when it comes to anything that smacks of self-help or personal development. His first inclination is to dismiss any new idea as "too simple," "too stupid," or "okay for other people," yet he's also oddly willing to give these things a try. (I suspect he does this so he can then reject them from firsthand experience!)

After the success of my first book, *You Can Have What You Want,* he asked me what my follow-up would be. When I told him that it was about how to feel happy, he seemed genuinely disappointed.

"Oh," he replied. "It's going to be one of *those* books."

I'm not sure exactly what he meant, but I asked him to try a little experiment. I suggested that he think about a problem he was having—a situation in his life where he was feeling slightly overwhelmed. When I noticed his eyes shift downward and his skin go a bit pale, I shouted, "Boo!" at him and he looked back up at me, startled but bemused.

Next I asked him to think a happy thought—to reflect on someone or something that made him smile. He seemed to find that a little bit harder, but he closed his eyes and concentrated. When I saw a grin forming on his lips and the color returning to his face, I guided him through the basic "Recipe for Feeling Good" exercise that I'll share with you in Chapter 3.

Soon he was breathing deeply and evenly, his shoulders were relaxed, and he had an expression of calm and peace on his face.

"Now," I said to him, "continuing to enjoy *these* feelings of ease and well-being, I want you to once again think about that situation you found overwhelming."

As I said the word *these,* I reached over and gently squeezed his shoulder, creating a simple association between that touch and his good feelings.

I watched his face as he began to think about the old situation in a brand-new way. The muscles around his eyes tensed, then relaxed, then tense again, then relaxed even more.

When he seemed completely at peace, I told him to open his eyes and asked him what had happened.

"That was weird," he answered. "When you asked me to think about a problem, I was going to focus on something at work, but then an image of my teenage daughter just popped into my head. We've been battling over pretty much everything for a while now, and I was just getting back into our most recent argument when you startled me."

He looked at me with a strange smile on his face.

"Then, when you asked me to think a happy thought, my mind went to my daughter again, but this time it was when she was a little girl. God, she could make me laugh! At first, I was just playing along with you, but it really did feel good to think about that so I gave myself over to the good feelings and just decided to enjoy it.

"When you squeezed my shoulder and asked me to go back and think about the problems that I'd been having with my daughter, it was really confusing . . . like I couldn't quite remember what it was about it that I'd been finding so difficult."

I then asked him, "So what's changed about your relationship with your daughter, just from having taken a few minutes out to feel happy before thinking about it again?"

His analytical mind kicked back in and he said dismissively, "Well, obviously, nothing's changed!"

Within a few moments, the smile returned to his eyes, as he continued somewhat reflectively, "But everything's different."

And this to me is the whole point of happiness (if indeed feeling happy needs "a point"):

> **When you're happy, nothing changes—**
> **but everything is different.**

"Mental mountains" are reduced to molehills; problems that seemed insoluble begin to dissolve in the light of your happy awareness. If there are things for you to do in order to make life more the way you want it to be, you have a remarkable sense of clarity about what to do and a remarkable sense of ease about actually doing it. In other words, your everyday routine may not look any different on the outside, but it feels completely transformed on the inside. And those new feelings of happiness are often the only difference you need to make all the difference in the world.

So if you're ready to feel happy now—even if you're not quite sure that it's really possible for you—let's get things started. . . .

PART I

Feeling Good

Chapter One

GETTING STARTED

The Three Myths of Happiness

"Myths which are believed in tend to become true."

— George Orwell

There are over 60,000 books in print at the moment on the subject of happiness, which is particularly interesting when you consider the fact that "happiness" doesn't even exist.

Like success, love, and confidence (not to mention stress, anxiety, and depression), the word *happiness* is what linguists call a "nominalization"—a process or activity that's described as if it were a tangible thing.

While the metaphor of happiness as a "thing" does make it easier to talk about, it also carries with it some interesting baggage.

If happiness were a thing:

- It could be lost or found outside of yourself.

- You could give it to or receive it from someone else.

- You could almost certainly buy it (and it would be cheaper and quicker to get on the Internet).

- You could share it with others.

This, of course, fits with the way that many of us think about happiness. But if our goal is to actually feel happy not only now, but more and more of the time, it's useful to regard "happiness" in terms of a process:

Happiness is the process of creating and experiencing good feelings in your body and mind, moment by moment by moment.

When you recognize happiness as a process, not a thing, you realize:

- You can do it or not do it.
- You can get better at it.
- You can ultimately master it.

More than 400 years ago, Francis Bacon wrote about what he called "the idols of the Western world": the ideas that are so much a part of our culture that we never think to question them, but instead worship them with the kind of blind faith normally reserved for religious rather than scientific pursuits.

I prefer to think of these ideas as myths—stories we tell ourselves about how the world works that are passed from generation to generation and never questioned until the moment we decide to value our own experience over and above the ideas before our minds.

Myth Number 1: "I'll Be Happy When . . ."

People tend to think that happiness is just around the corner and will miraculously arrive the moment they get their act together, achieve all of their goals, find the man or woman of their dreams, and attain spiritual enlightenment. But is it really true?

Have you ever reached a goal or gotten something you always wanted, only to find that within a few months, weeks, or even moments, the thrill was gone and you were back to searching for that elusive something that would fill the hole and fulfill your longing for something greater?

If all there was to happiness was getting what you wanted, the richest and most outwardly successful people in our society would be the happiest. However, it only takes a quick glance through the pages of today's newspapers and magazines before you're reading about the latest miserable millionaire or celebrity scandal.

The reality is simply this:

> *Your happiness does not depend on*
> *getting or having what you want.*

When we step out from behind the myth and become willing to pursue happiness directly, we also become free to move joyously forward in the direction of our goals and dreams.

Myth Number 2: It's Not Possible to Be Happy in Certain Situations

The idea that our happiness and well-being in life are the products of our circumstances seems to be self-evident at first glance. After all, isn't everybody sad at a funeral? And when's the last time you saw a group of sports fans celebrating after their team lost a big game?

But in the same way that the presence of fire engines at the scene of a blaze doesn't mean that fire engines cause fires, the regular presence of unhappiness in certain situations doesn't mean the situation caused the unhappiness.

The truth behind this myth is a subtle one:

While it may or may not be possible to be happy all the time, it is certainly possible to be happy at any time.

In fact, each one of the situations you think of as "making" you unhappy is simply an area of your life in which you think that it would be inappropriate to feel happy (for example, at a funeral) or that feeling happy would be in some way bad for you. (Don't worry if that doesn't make sense to you just yet—we'll talk more about it later!)

Myth Number 3: Unhappiness Is Good for Us

It's undeniable that unhappiness is a part of life, and many philosophers and scientists point to the evolutionary role that fear and anger have played in the survival of the species. But when we start to justify our bad feelings as being good for us (or, worse still, our good feelings as being bad for us), we keep ourselves stuck in a self-fulfilling rut.

Ironically, the state of discomfort that most of us put ourselves in to better deal with our problems is the worst possible state in which to deal with them. Like pouring fuel on a fire, meeting difficulties with anger, fear, and sadness tends to make things more . . . well . . . difficult.

Here's what's waiting for us on the other side of this myth:

> *Whatever you can do with unhappiness,*
> *you can do better when you're happy.*

As long as we justify our unhappiness as being necessary and important, we'll make sure that we have more of it. The moment we recognize that our chief aims in life are almost entirely achievable with positive emotion, we can change the very basis of our lives.

The Happy Formula

There are three main things you need to learn and practice in order to feel happy—not only now, but whenever you want to for the rest of your life:

1. Give yourself better feelings.
2. Tell yourself better stories.
3. Act on your inner knowing.

These three steps make up what I call "the happy formula" and correspond to the three areas of happiness discussed in ancient and modern philosophy: emotional happiness (feelings), judgmental happiness (stories), and moral happiness (right action). As you learn to feel, think, and act happily in the world, you'll find that each skill builds on the one before, ultimately forming a wonderfully joyful circle:

- The better you feel, the better stories you tend to tell yourself about your life.

- The better stories you tell yourself about your life, the easier it is to do what you know is right for you.

- The more you do what you know is right for you, the better you feel.

In other words, the better you feel in your body, the easier it is to practice the skills that create the internal and external environments that foster happiness. And practice works for anyone, no matter where or when you start.

The Stupid Thumb

When I was a child, there was a rumor going around the school yard that if the wrong thumb was on top when you clasped your hands with interlacing fingers, it meant that you were stupid.

While I no longer remember which one it was, I was horrified to discover that I had the "stupid" thumb. I immediately made plans to pack up all my worldly belongings into a small shopping bag and head for the hills, where people with all kinds of thumbs could live together in peace and harmony. However, after a long and heartfelt talk with my favorite stuffed animal, I decided that rather than run away, I'd face my demons and force my thumbs to behave like the intelligent digits I knew them to be.

I embarked on a program of conditioning my body to behave in a new way. Each morning I'd consciously interlace my fingers at least 100 times, being sure to place the "nonstupid" thumb on top. When I first started, it felt incredibly odd to connect my hands in the "wrong" way, but after only a few mornings, it began to feel more and more natural. At some point in the first two weeks, I closed my eyes and brought my hands together. When I opened my eyes and looked down, the new thumb was on top!

I had done it—I'd changed what felt "normal" and comfortable simply by consciously repeating a new behavior on a regular basis. And despite the fact that I now recognize that the only thing it had to do with my level of intelligence was that I believed it, I did learn an important lesson in the process:

You become what you practice.

Whatever we do consistently (that is, practice), we get better at. If we practice anger, we get better at being angry; if we practice shutting down our emotions, we get better at feeling depressed. And if we practice giving ourselves better feelings, telling ourselves better stories, and acting on our inner knowing, we'll get better and better at feeling happy.

The question is, what are you practicing *now?*

Chapter Two

THE ART AND SCIENCE OF DELIGHT

How to Feel Sad

> *"The first and simplest emotion which we discover
> in the human mind is curiosity."*
> — Edmund Burke

When my son was six, I walked into his bedroom one day and found him all teary eyed, snuggled up in the arms of a giant teddy bear named Harvey. When I asked why he was upset, he said, "I was thinking about my friend Thomas and how we're not really friends anymore because he's mean to me."

Although I was tempted to interrupt and congratulate my son for setting strong boundaries at such a tender age, I bit my tongue and asked, "Is that why you're sad?"

"No," he replied, seeming genuinely surprised at the thought. "I'm sad because if I think really, really hard about how much fun we could have been having if we were still friends, it makes me cry."

With tears in my eyes, I had to agree with him—that was, indeed, an excellent way to make yourself unhappy.

The truth is, I can remember the day he first figured out the mechanics of feeling sad. One night our cat, Mason, was run over in front of our house. The next morning, my then three-year-old son was excitedly telling everybody all about the gross thing that had happened to his cat. By the end of the day, having successfully gauged the reactions of the grown-ups around him, he had learned to tell the story in a "sad voice" and act it out with pursed lips, hunched shoulders, and downcast eyes.

So, if you want to feel sad, here's a simple three-step recipe:

1. Think really, really hard about things that upset you.

2. Talk about them in a "sad voice."

3. Purse your lips (you can cry if you want), hunch your shoulders, and shift your gaze downward.

Why this works so well is easy to understand if you take a closer look at how we create our personal experience of any given moment. There are essentially three variables that comprise the structure of our subjective experience:

1. The way we use our body
2. The maps we make in our head
3. The stories we tell ourselves

This model was first developed by Dr. Richard Bandler in the field of Neuro-Linguistic Programming (NLP), and it can be used to make sense of how we create all of our experiences. Let's examine each of these three elements in more detail:

1. The Way We Use Our Body

An exercise that I used to conduct at the beginning of my trainings was to ask each person in the group to stand tall, look up toward the ceiling, put on a big toothy grin—and then feel depressed!

No matter how long they stood there, if they continued standing straight and tall, gazing upward with an embarrassingly silly, toothy grin on their faces, they found themselves utterly unable to depress themselves. (They were, however, often capable of making themselves extremely angry with me afterward for asking them to do something so silly!)

You can test the connection between how you use your body and how you feel inside right now.

> Go ahead and sit the way you'd be sitting if reading this book were the most boring thing that you've ever had to do. (Hopefully, you shifted your body in some way—if not, stop reading immediately and go get yourself a different book!)
>
> Now move so that you're sitting in the way you would be sitting if you were curious about what I was about to say—in the same way that you might be curious about what was inside your presents on your birthday. . . .
>
> Finally, shift your body until you're sitting the way you would be sitting if you knew that the very next thing I'll tell you is the key to a lifetime of happiness, enabling you to achieve all of your most important goals and single-handedly bring about world peace. . . .
>
> Got it?
>
> Good.
>
> Now stay that way as you read through the rest of this book!

While I'm obviously not expecting you to actually do this, it's interesting to think about how much more enjoyable your experience might be if you decide to give it a try. . . .

2. The Maps We Make in Our Head

In order to make sense of the world, we re-present the information we take in through our five senses inside our mind—that is, we make an internal representation of the data, sort of like an inner map. We then make decisions and choose our actions based on those inner maps.

Of course, in order to make a map, you need to leave things out (otherwise, it would be as large as the territory), make generalizations (all water is blue, all parks are green, and so on), and distort perspectives so that everything fits. This is what makes a map useful, but it's also what creates problems.

Here's the key:

What we perceive to be problems in our lives has nothing to do with what is happening in the world and everything to do with the limitations of our mental maps.

When you understand this, you'll know that changing your mind—your map—can literally change your life.

If a picture is worth 1,000 words, take a look at this one. . . .

Think of a (small) problem you've been having. It can be one you've been dealing with for a long time or one that has just come up. (I love brand-new problems—they're so shiny!) Notice where in space you represent the problem. If you're not sure, just point to where you think it might be.

Next, notice if you're looking at the problem through your own eyes or if you can see yourself in the image. Is it moving or still? Clear or fuzzy? Large or small?

Now, if you were looking through your own eyes, step out of the picture so that you can see yourself in it, like you can see yourself in a photograph. Push the image a comfortable distance away. If it was moving (like a film), make it still (like a snapshot); if it was clear, make it fuzzy; and if it was large, shrink it down until it's the size of a postage stamp. Then stick it on an envelope and mail it to someone who you think can handle it. I'll wait. . . .

Now think about the "problem" again. Does it feel less significant than it did before you began? If not, continue to play with the details of your representation until you've given yourself a useful new perspective.

3. The Stories We Tell Ourselves

The third structure we use to create subjective experiences is language. Language is another mapping tool—one we use to create, describe, and share our experiences with one another. We do this primarily by telling ourselves and others around us stories about what we've experienced.

In a recent cover story from *New Scientist* magazine, Helen Phillips wrote:

> There is certainly plenty of evidence that much of what we do is the result of unconscious brain processing, and that our consciousness seems to be interpreting what has happened, rather than driving it. . . .
>
> Our senses may take in more than 11 million pieces of information each second, whereas even the most liberal estimates suggest that we are conscious of just 40 of these. . . .
>
> It is an unsettling thought that perhaps all our conscious mind ever does is dream up stories in an attempt to make sense of our world.

This new research supports the idea that it's the unconscious mind that drives most of an individual's decisions and behavior. Even our memories aren't really real, but rather maps and stories that we've constructed with internal images, sounds, and feelings in order to "make sense" of our experiences.

Together, all of these elements—the way we use our body, the internal maps we make, and the stories we tell ourselves about why and how we're doing it—create our neurophysiological state.

Since feeling good is a particularly useful (and pleasant) neurophysiological state, it's worth learning to adapt your physiology, representations, and stories in order to create this state inside of you.

Take a moment now to do this for yourself. . . .

Creating a Good Feeling

1. Notice how you're feeling in your body right now.

2. Shift your body until you're feeling just a little bit better. You could do this by sitting up straighter, getting up and gently stretching, smiling up into your eyes and down into your body, or you can simply take a deep breath and feel it spread into every part of yourself.

3. Next, speak to yourself in a friendly voice. Give yourself a sincere compliment, or remember a time where you received praise for something that you did. Enjoy the good feelings that come with "hearing" those positive words.

4. Make a picture of yourself in your mind, and imagine how you'd look if you were just a little bit happier than you are right now. When you've got it, step into the picture and enjoy the good feelings.

5. Repeat each of the previous steps until you've successfully created a smile on your face and a good feeling in your body!

In order to better understand why this technique works so well, let's explore a little bit of the science behind it. . . .

The Chemistry of Happiness

> *"Everything should be made as simple as possible,*
> *but no simpler."*
> — Albert Einstein

According to the latest research in the science of emotion, every feeling we have in our body is a "neurochemical event." That is, every time we perceive something in the world and then interpret it in our brains, certain chemicals are released into our bodies. When everything is working perfectly, just the right amounts of just the right chemicals are released to put our bodies into an optimal state for whatever action is required.

For example, if you were to walk out of your cave one morning and encounter an angry woolly mammoth on the way to work, your brain would no doubt interpret this as a danger and trigger the release of adrenaline and cortisol into your body. These chemicals would cause you to narrow your focus, sharpen your thinking, empty your bowels, temporarily increase your strength (like Popeye's spinach!), and prepare you to either fight the mammoth or run like hell in the opposite direction.

When it comes to happiness, there are two different chemicals that we're interested in:

1. Dopamine

Dopamine is the "motivation chemical." The release of dopamine into the bloodstream increases our ability to focus and motivates us to take action. Dopamine levels naturally rise as we move toward a goal and begin to anticipate a result. They tend to be at their highest when we're in active pursuit of getting our most basic needs met.

2. Serotonin

Serotonin is the "feel-good chemical," and is as calming and soothing as dopamine is energizing. When dopamine produces effort, serotonin provides the reward.

We receive an increase in serotonin whenever we:

- Win anything, from a game of tic-tac-toe to the lottery

- Get public recognition for a job well done

- Take certain drugs or drink alcohol

- Feel like part of a crowd, group, or team (for example, at a football game or a book club)

Together, the interplay of dopamine and serotonin make the world go round. Higher levels of dopamine move us forward; higher levels of serotonin provide feelings of safety, satisfaction, and curiosity.

When looked at through this chemical filter, we can understand the innate appeal of goal-driven behavior, whether it's trying to do a Sudoku puzzle or change the world. We not only get the energized, focused sensations that come from the buildup of dopamine in trying to solve the puzzle or reach the goal; we also get the calm, contented feelings of satisfaction and well-being that follow the release of serotonin at the moment of triumph and success.

We can also understand why it's imperative to get

our brain chemistry firing on all cylinders. One recent study showed that in autopsies of more than 63 people who had committed suicide over the course of a year, a common factor was a complete lack of serotonin in the bloodstream.

In other words, when the serotonin goes, the will to live can go with it. But when you fill your brain with happy chemicals, you feel good in your body now and optimistic about the future.

While there are certain pharmaceutical drugs and natural remedies that have been shown to increase the body's stores of serotonin (and others that block and limit it), they lie outside of the scope of this book. Instead, we're interested in how we can release "happy chemicals" into our bloodstream on demand, using nothing more than our understanding, attention, and intention.

And in order to do that, we need to take a look at a third chemical, closely linked to serotonin but with some wonderfully unique properties all its own. . . .

The Nectar of the Gods

"You would then reach into your bag and pull out a Fuzzy the size of a child's hand. As soon as the Fuzzy saw the light of day it would smile and blossom into a large, shaggy Warm Fuzzy. When you laid the Warm Fuzzy on the person's head, shoulder or lap it would snuggle up and melt right against their skin and make them feel good all over."
— from *A Warm Fuzzy Tale,* by Claude M. Steiner

In the early 1970s, a graduate student named Candace Pert discovered that every cell in our body contained what she called "opiate receptors." She found that these receptors were particularly in tune with one special kind of chemical messenger called "endogenous morphines," more commonly known as "endorphins." Endorphins (or, as my four-year-old calls them, "en-dolphins") are the body's natural opiates, the neurotransmitters that control pain and create pleasure. They're the biochemical source of that happy, glowing feeling that Claude Steiner calls the "Warm Fuzzy."

Whenever you feel a warm glow after sex, the sweet sensation of looking at a cute puppy or baby, or even the release and relaxation of climbing into a warm bath at the end of a hard day, what you're experiencing are endorphins swimming happily through your bloodstream.

You get a natural endorphin release when you exercise, make love, laugh a lot, and relax deeply. And not only does the presence of endorphins make you feel better, but it can make you smarter and more capable as well. As Paul McKenna says in his book *Change Your Life in 7 Days:*

> Because endorphins are neuro-transmitters, they create more bonding in the brain, so every time you experience an endorphin release, they actually make you more intelligent. And every cell in your body has receptors for endorphins. How great a design feature is that? Not only can every cell in our body experience happiness, but the more often we choose to be happy, the more intelligent we become!
>
> The best thing about understanding the phenomenal role of endorphins in our health, happiness and wellbeing is that we don't have to wait for spontaneous releases of endorphins in order to experience their benefits—we can cultivate the endorphin response through practice.

Let's do a quick experiment so you can experience this for yourself:

> Imagine that your body is filled with golden light. (It can actually be whatever color you like—any color that brings a smile to your face when you think about it.)
>
> Now imagine that light flowing throughout your body like a warm liquid, nourishing every cell and organ along the way.
>
> If you look closely, you can see tiny little "en-dolphins" swimming in the light. Each en-dolphin is a carrier of joy.
>
> Imagine yourself diving into the light and swimming with the en-dolphins. You can continue doing this for as long as it feels good. . . .

Soon you'll find that just thinking about swimming with your own endorphins will bring a wave of good feelings to your body and mind! The more you practice, the easier it becomes.

A Measure of Happiness

In order to better evaluate the benefits of this "happy practice" over time, I'd like to propose the use of an extremely simple measure—what researchers call a "subjective happiness scale":

> How happy are you feeling right now on a scale from 1 to 10, where 1 is the most horrible feeling

you can imagine and 10 is the most wonderful one?

Don't worry about what the number is or how it might compare to the numbers of the people around you—we'll only be using this scale to compare you to you.

Now answer this question: What could you do right now to take yourself up the "subjective happiness scale" by one (that is, from a 3 to a 4 or an 8 to a 9)?

Have a quick think, and then do whatever it is—you can continue reading when you've bumped yourself up at least one number on the scale. . . .

What did you do? Did you take a deep breath and smile? Think a happy thought? Think about someone you love or someone (or something) who loves you?

Perhaps you got up and stretched or jotted down a brief note to get something out of your head so you could be fully present to what you're reading now.

If you got stuck (or just skipped ahead without playing along!), try this instead: Take yourself down the subjective happiness scale by one: from 10 to 9, 7 to 6, or even 2 to 1. I'll wait. . . .

What did you do?

Did you think about something you've been worrying about and haven't been able to get out of your head? Did you create pictures of bad things happening to people whom you care about, or tell yourself scary stories about something that might not work out in your favor? (Or, worse still, how terrible you are at doing exercises like this?)

> Okay, one last experiment . . .
>
> Imagine what it would be like to live your entire life at an 8, 9, or 10. Really step into your imagination and think about being truly, deeply happy in the kinds of situations you normally encounter at work, with friends, and at home. Imagine feeling the way you feel when things are really wonderful.
>
> Would people notice? Would they wonder what had happened to you?

If you do nothing else in this book but practice releasing your endorphins and feeling good on a regular basis, it will make a tremendous difference to the quality of your life. And as you've probably begun to experience, creating feelings of happiness in your body is surprisingly simple to do. What can be more difficult is allowing those happy feelings to permeate your life.

We'll take a look at why that is and what you can do about it in the next chapter. . . .

Chapter Three

<u>HAPPINESS RULES</u>

The Permission Principle

> *"Most people are about as happy as they
> make their minds up to be."*
> — Abraham Lincoln

When would "now" be a good time to feel happy?

Contrary to what you may think, the number one obstacle to your happiness isn't your job, your significant other, the weather, the time of the month, or even the state of the economy. It's your own willingness to feel happy in spite of all these things.

To put it another way, the reason you're not feeling happy now (if, indeed, you aren't feeling happy now) is simply because at some level, it's not okay with you to do so until you've sorted out:

- Your moods
- Your bank balance
- Your relationship(s)
- Your clutter
- Your weight
- Your "bad" habits
- Your life

This is what I call "the permission principle":

You will feel happy in direct proportion to your willingness to feel happy without anything in your life changing from how it is right now.

The reason why more people aren't happier more of the time isn't because they can't be—it's because they think they shouldn't be. And if you don't think it's okay for you to feel happy right now, it isn't all that likely that you will.

What you're up against is that voice inside your head that goes a little something like this:

> *It's not okay for me to feel happy now because something in my life isn't quite right (although I'm not necessarily sure exactly what that is). I need to stay unsettled and at least slightly uncomfortable until I've dealt with whatever it is that's not quite right. I must remain in a state of heightened awareness to remind myself that there's something I need to deal with in the future.*

The problem is that our definition of "not quite right" is almost unfathomably broad.

Why Are You Unhappy?

In her book *Composing a Life,* Mary Catherine Bateson shares the story of a conversation she had as a young child with her father, the famous British anthropologist Gregory Bateson. According to Mary Catherine, she was unhappy because everything on her desk was always messed up. Her father asked how she knew it was "messed up"; and she responded by explaining that her ruler wasn't in a straight line parallel to her blotter, which wasn't equidistant from the corners of her desk . . . and don't even get her started about the arrangement and relative sharpness of her pencils!

After several minutes of this, her father replied: "The reason everything always seems to be so messed up is because there is only one way for things to be right, but over 1,000 ways they can be messed up."

Most of us have designed our lives in the exact same fashion. We have thousands and thousands of ways our lives can be messed up, the vast majority of which are completely outside of our control. This puts us firmly at the mercy of circumstance in a world where most people's circumstances aren't really known for being merciful. Consequently, we only give ourselves permission to feel truly happy in those all-too-rare moments when the fates align and all of our conditions for happiness are mysteriously (and temporarily) met.

How specifically do you know when it's okay (or not okay) to feel happy now? In most cases, it's by consulting the "rule book" in your head—and since you didn't consciously choose most of the rules, you may find that they begin to change as they come up into your conscious awareness.

Let's take a look at a few of them right now. . . .

1. Write down a list of situations in which you think it would be uncomfortable, inappropriate, or "just plain wrong" to feel happy. For example:

- A funeral
- After losing a big game
- When your partner is mad at you

2. Now make a list of "approved" situations when feeling happy "makes sense" to you. For example:

- A wedding
- After winning a big game
- When your partner is happy with you

3. For each of the "just plain wrong" situations, ask yourself the following questions:

- *Why would it be wrong to feel happy in this situation?*

- *What am I concerned it would mean about me if I felt happy in this situation?*

- *What am I afraid I would or wouldn't do if I felt happy in this situation?*

Once you recognize the role that permission plays in your pursuit of happiness, you'll see that there are really only three questions you need to answer before you can fully engage in the process of becoming "unreasonably happy":

- *Do I want to feel happy now?*
- *Am I willing to feel happy now?*
- *How can I feel happy now?*

Without taking the time to answer the first two questions, there's almost no point in answering the third. With the exception of extreme depression and anxiety, feeling happy is more often a matter of "will" or "won't" than "can" or "can't."

Over the next few pages, I'll share a simple three-step process that will enable you to feel happy in your body regardless of what's going on in your world.

As you practice these techniques over time, you're retraining your nervous system to experience a fairly steady flow of endorphins through your body on an ongoing basis. The more you do so, the more good feelings you'll be able to handle. What's now your 10 will become a 1 as you gain access to levels of bliss and well-being that you may not yet be able to imagine.

Before long, you'll begin to be "overcome by good feelings" even when you haven't been consciously practicing them: during a movie, while walking in the park, or even in the middle of a crowded supermarket. And the more often you allow yourself to feel good, the better you get to feel.

A Recipe for Feeling Good

In the same way that a recipe tells you exactly what you need to do to prepare a meal but allows you a great deal of scope and sway in how you do it, I'd now like to introduce you to a three-step recipe for happiness and well-being that you can cook up in the midst of any circumstance or situation.

Here are the steps in a nutshell:

1. Go to your heart and trigger a good feeling.

2. Crank up the intensity of the good feeling and spread it throughout your body.

3. Focus on the positive benefits of feeling this way both now and in the future.

Let's go through each of these in a bit more detail. If you'd like, you can actually do each step as you read about it now. . . .

1. Go to your heart and trigger a good feeling. According to research done by the Institute of HeartMath, your emotional states are reflected in your heart rhythms. When you create greater coherence in your heart rhythms (by focusing attention on your physical heart and awakening feelings of love and appreciation), your emotional states will follow suit.

Specifically, what I'd like you to do is this:

> Place at least one hand on your chest, covering your heart. Now take three slow and gentle breaths into your heart. Think about someone you love or someone who loves you until you begin to feel the release of endorphins—like a warm, fuzzy feeling in the very center of your chest.

2. Crank up the intensity of the good feeling and spread it throughout your body. Once you've triggered a good feeling, your next step is to turn it up and spread it throughout your body. There are many ways to do this, but here are a few of my favorites. Don't worry if they don't all work for you the first time—just choose the one that seems best for now and go for it!

a. Picture the good feeling in your heart as your favorite color. The more vividly you see it, the better the feeling gets. Visualize the color like a bucket of paint dripping throughout your entire body, from the top of your head all the way down to the tips of your toes.

b. Imagine that the good feeling in your heart is like a warm liquid or golden honey. Experiment until you find just the right temperature inside. Then taste and feel the warm honeylike liquid as it spreads throughout every cell of your body.

c. Experience the good feeling in your heart like a gentle, tingling energy. Notice that you can speed up this sensation or slow it down until it feels absolutely wonderful. Now direct this wonderful energy until you can feel your whole body tingling.

3. Focus on the positive benefits of feeling this way both now and in the future. In order to take full advantage of the good feeling that's hopefully dancing inside your body right now, decide that it's not only okay to feel happy in this moment, but it will also be good for you in the future.

Here are a few simple ways to do this now:

While bathing in the healing bliss of your own flow of endorphins, think about the fact that your nervous system is actively repairing itself and recovering from the stresses and strains of daily life.

Rest in the awareness that each time you allow yourself to "cook up" these good feelings inside your body, you're creating and strengthening neural pathways in your brain that are making it easier and more natural for you to feel happy in the future.

Imagine how much easier the challenges of your life will be when you return to them having taken this time-out to refresh your body and recharge your mind. . . .

Happy Practice

While in theory happiness makes us feel wonderful, in practice it enables us to create a more and more wonderful life. The three tools we use to build our happiness—the way we use our body, the maps we make in our minds, and the stories we tell ourselves—are the same tools we employ to make ourselves miserable.

Once you master the process, you get to choose the result. And before long, you'll recognize something very important:

> *The only thing between you and feeling*
> *happy now is a story.*

In the next section of this book, I'll share some of the techniques I've learned to not only reduce uncomfortable feelings in any moment, but also to build up reserves of positive feelings that will carry you through the most difficult circumstances with ease and grace.

Until then, let's ponder the story of a seeker who wanted to know more about being truly happy. . . .

A master of happiness was traveling with a cumbersome bag upon his shoulder when he came across a seeker. The seeker asked him what true happiness really felt like.

The master paused for a moment, then smiled and took the bag off his shoulder. As it dropped heavily to the ground, he stood tall in the freedom from the burden he'd been carrying.

The seeker said, "I think I understand. And what do you do once you're happy?"

The master smiled, hoisted his bag, and carried on down the road.

When you're ready to carry on down the road, I'll be waiting for you in the next chapter!

PART II

Feeling
Better

Chapter Four

WHAT'S YOUR STORY?

The Facts of Life

*"I am a lover of what is, not because I'm a spiritual person,
but because it hurts when I argue with reality."*
— Byron Katie

One morning I went outside and saw that some builders had dumped wet concrete on my lawn during the "cleanup" after a job. Big problem—the lawn was newly seeded and the concrete had now mixed with the dirt and hardened. I was probably going to have to dig up the lawn and start over. My mind began to race as I considered the many things that I'd need to do in order to fix the problem and perhaps "fix" the builders in the process.

In the midst of quietly—and not so quietly—fuming about it, I received a call from a client whose father was on his way to having an "inoperable" brain tumor operated on by some surgeons who fortunately forgot to read the manual about what can't be done.

When I returned outside about 20 minutes later, I noticed with interest that there was still some concrete on my lawn. What had changed was that it was no longer a problem—it had returned to just being concrete.

In order to make something into a "problem," you have to do one of two things:

1.   Compare it to how things used to be and decide they should be that way again, even though they aren't.

2.   Compare it to how you'd like it to be and decide it should be that way now, even though it's not.

In other words, to turn a fact of life into a problem to be solved, you first have to create a story about how things should be instead.

I remember when my parents dropped me off at the airport before I first moved to England at the age of 20. I was excited about the trip and couldn't wait to get on the plane. I was about to begin a new chapter in my life—the story of an actor striving to make his mark in the footsteps of Edmund Kean, Laurence Olivier, and Albert Finney. It wasn't until I saw my parents' palpable sadness as they walked away from the departure gate that it occurred to me they, too, were beginning a new chapter, but their story was about an aging couple whose last child was fleeing the nest. Same event, completely different experience.

The Making of Meaning

Our story is the meaning that we give to the facts of our lives—our interpretation of reality. If we make the facts mean good things about us and the future, we'll feel happy about them; if we make them mean bad things, we'll feel unhappy about them. Either way, we're the ones making the meaning.

During my live trainings, I often do an exercise with participants where I invite them to come up with multiple meanings for a significant life event by repeatedly asking the question, "What else could this mean?"

For example, if someone says their husband or wife has left them, most people will assume that's a bad thing and respond accordingly with a blend of sympathy and encouragement. But what else could it mean?

Here are some typical answers from seminar participants—notice that some make it a good thing, some a bad thing, and others are relatively neutral:

- *"Now they're free to meet someone who's <u>really</u> right for them."*

- *"They'll never meet anyone else, and they'll be alone—and miserable—for the rest of their lives."*

- *"What they learn from the experience will make them a more loving partner in the future."*

- *"They're scarred for life and will never experience love again."*

- *"It's an opportunity to fight to win their partner back."*

- *"It's life's way of saying, 'Time to move on.'"*

After a few rounds of the game, it becomes clear that it's possible to make up hundreds of different meanings for any given event. The more optimistic the meaning, the better the accompanying feelings; the less optimistic, the worse the story feels. But when you've played the game long enough, a new, even more useful question emerges:

What do you want it to mean?

When you realize that you're literally making up the meaning of even the most significant "facts" of your life, you can deliberately choose the meanings that feel good and empower positive action. As I say to my clients:

**If you're going to make stuff up,
make up good stuff.**

The way to consistently "make up good stuff" is to understand and master what cognitive psychologists call your "explanatory style."

In his research into pessimism, optimism, depression, and happiness, Dr. Martin Seligman noticed that people who tended to define bad things as permanent, personal, and pervasive had a completely different life experience from those who explained their problems as being temporary, specific, and impersonal.

I'd been teaching the idea of explanatory style for several years before I really experienced the full power of it for myself. One of my students was a medical doctor, and I called him for advice the morning I was due to make a presentation at Regent's College in London. My stomach ached, my head was killing me, and I felt like I was going to die.

Inside, I was telling myself a dramatic story about how I should have taken better care of myself (personal), and being sick meant that I was an irresponsible person (pervasive). In addition, I could imagine myself throwing up during the presentation, getting kicked out of the college, and being told never to darken their doors again (permanent).

When I asked the doctor what he thought I should do, he went through a few diagnostic questions with me and then replied that it sounded as though I had the "three-hour flu," which apparently could strike anyone. If I was willing to ride it out, I'd feel better within a few hours. In fact, I felt better the moment I got off the phone. Although I wasn't at my best, I got through the presentation with ease.

It was only afterward, when I thought about what had happened, that I called my doctor friend back. When I questioned him about it, he somewhat sheepishly admitted that he'd made up the three-hour flu diagnosis. He knew from my description of symptoms that I wasn't dangerously ill, but he also knew he couldn't make me well in the few minutes we had together over the phone.

He said he could tell I was making things worse with the scary stories I was telling myself, so he quickly reviewed our class notes while I was talking and made up an explanation for the bad feelings in my body that was impersonal, temporary, and specific.

I'm not sure to this day which one of us was more surprised that it had actually worked!

Try this simple experiment in shifting your "explanatory style." It's easiest to do it on paper, but you can also go through it aloud with a friend.

Why Things Are the Way They Are

1. Think of a situation in your life that went badly. Now answer the question, "Why did it go badly?" as if you were explaining it to a friend.

2. Once again, tell the story of why it went badly, but this time take out any reference to it being your fault in any way. (This is the first *p:* personalization.)

3. Now explain what happened again, but retell it as if it were a random, one-time occurrence with a beginning, middle, and end. (This is the second *p:* permanence.)

4. Finally, explain the situation as if it were an isolated down point in the otherwise awesome panorama of positivity that is your life! (This is the third *p:* pervasiveness.)

5. Notice which of the three shifts (personalization, permanence, or pervasiveness) made the biggest impact on your state of mind, and begin to rewrite the stories of your life from this new and different point of view.

The wonderful thing about being able to change the meanings of your life and shift your explanatory style is that your story begins to loosen its hold over your experience. In fact, if I were going to nominate one key factor in both the success of my business and my marriage, it would be my recognition of the reality that my story is just a story and doesn't need to be given much weight. Therefore, while my default thinking about things can at times be quite pessimistic, it doesn't have the hold over my behavior that it would if I really believed it.

Challenging your stories of impending doom isn't only powerful, it's fun—and it serves as an ongoing reminder that no matter how detailed or practiced your story is, it's still only a story. The question is, who's telling it?

Meeting the Storyteller

Nearly everyone I've ever met or worked with experiences a voice or set of voices in their head that seems to have an opinion about everything they do, don't do, or even think about doing or not doing. (And if you think you don't have a voice inside your head, isn't it a voice inside your head telling you that?)

I call this collection of inner voices "the storyteller." Your inner storyteller is the narrator of your life, translating what you see and hear and feel into descriptions, assessments, judgments, and observations. It began doing this at an early age, turning the facts of your life into stories to be told and problems to be solved.

Now if you listen very carefully, you may hear your mind trying to turn what I've just said into a problem— either by thinking you don't have a storyteller or that having one is bad and wrong. The part of your mind that's either agreeing with or questioning what I've just said is the storyteller in action!

Here are some ideas you can put into practice immediately that will help you create a more positive relationship with your inner storyteller:

1. Write it down. When I'm working on things that are outside my comfort zone, my inner storyteller kicks into overdrive. What I've noticed is that if I stay engaged in the activity long enough, the voice goes quiet.

One day, just for fun, I decided to catalog the many things that my inner voice had to say about why I should give up on a project I was working on:

- Variations on "I want to quit" = 4

- Variations on "I can't do this" = 6

- Variations on "I hate this business/life/myself/ etc." = 12

- Variations on "I'm not good enough/I'm not worthy/I suck/etc." = 16

By simply writing these things down as they came up, I was able to hear each thought without buying into its message. That gave me the freedom to give myself some better feelings and carry on working on the task at hand.

2. Move it around. One technique that works extremely well when your inner storyteller is speaking in "you" messages instead of "I" messages (for example, *"You're* a loser," *"You* can't do this," or "Who do *you* think *you're* kidding?") is to change its location.

First, notice where you currently hear your storyteller's voice: Is it at the back of your head? Whispering in your ear? Screaming in your temples?

Next, experiment with putting it in the very center of your throat, as if you were about to say out loud whatever it says in your head. People often report that when they do this, the message changes from a "you" to an "I," and the voice shifts from an individual in your past (often a critical parent or teacher) to your own.

Finally, place the voice outside of your body where you can have a dialogue with it from a comfortable distance. (If you ever see me having an animated conversation with my big toe, you'll know why!)

3. Re-dub it. Have you ever noticed that Mickey Mouse always plays the hero?

One of the reasons why he has so scrupulously maintained his "squeaky clean" image is that it would be very difficult for anyone to take him seriously as a villain. Imagine Mickey Mouse as Dracula, attempting to terrify the heroine by shouting out in a high-pitched Transylvanian accent, "I've come to drink your blood!" Or what if Mickey had replaced Arnold Schwarzenegger in *The Terminator* and had to squeak the immortal words, "I'll be back!"

In fact, that voice inside your head always seems so reasonable and compelling because it sounds just like you. By re-dubbing your inner dialogue in the voice of your favorite cartoon character, you can create a completely different experience.

Imagine Sylvester the cat complaining, "Nobody understands me!" Or Elmer Fudd bemoaning, "I'm sooooo depressed." Not only would you not take their stories seriously, you'd laugh at how ridiculous they sounded. And in that space of laughter, you'd potentially be able to help them change their story.

4. Comfort it. One of my most successful clients swears by telling that voice inside his head to "#%@! off" at every opportunity. For those of you who, like me, find that a bit harsh, "Thank you for sharing" works nicely, as does my personal variation—a gentle, soothing "Shhhhh . . ." as if you were comforting a distraught child.

Here are a few ways of practicing these techniques and integrating them into your day. . . .

Mastering the Storyteller

1. Throughout the day today, listen for your inner storyteller—"that voice inside your head." Jot down what you hear as you hear it. At the end of the day, look for any patterns in the kinds of things you've written down. If there's something that has a strong emotional charge, take the time to make up some new meanings and shift your explanatory style.

2. The next time you go to the movies (or are watching a film on TV), alternate between losing yourself in the world of the film and "coming back to your senses," reminding yourself that "it's just a movie." When you get good at this, do the same thing with your inner thoughts and stories.

---

3. Experiment with moving your critical self-talk to different locations outside of your head. It can also help to externalize it by saying it out loud.

4. Imagine that you have a volume control for the voices inside your head. If you're not aware of any voices, notice what happens if you turn the volume right up loud and then all the way down until you're left with the experience of true quiet.

5. Which voice does your inner storyteller use when it *really* wants you to pay attention? Write out a list of positive compliments about yourself and have your storyteller read it to you in *that* tone of voice.

6. Make a list of all the things that you know would take you in the direction of your biggest dream. If that voice inside your head begins to scream, practice re-dubbing it with the voice of your favorite cartoon character.

7. Finally, if all else fails, just say "Shhhhh!"

A Little Piece of Quiet

When my inner storyteller wants to entertain, amuse, or even frighten me, one of its favorite stories to tell about me is this one. . . .

I was about to head out to an important meeting. I was feeling incredibly organized and even a little bit smug about having given myself two hours to get there, which was more than twice as long as it would probably take me. Having carefully gone through my portfolio to make sure that I had everything I needed for the meeting, I went out to the car, put my things in the back, sat down in the driver's seat . . . and then realized I didn't have the car keys.

Not a problem. Back into the house I went. For almost an hour. No keys. Anywhere.

Finally, with time running out, it dawned on me that my wife had a spare set in her handbag. Relieved (and a little cross with myself for not having thought of that earlier), I grabbed the keys, ran back out to the car, started it up, and drove off to my meeting.

Before I'd driven 100 feet, I began to panic. There was a strange clanking noise coming from outside the driver's side window. Worried that I might have a flat tire, I pulled over, got out, and found the source of the noise. It was my original set of keys, still sitting in the lock of the car door, right where I'd left them more than an hour earlier.

So why did that happen? How was it possible for me not to notice my keys sitting in the door of the car as I searched frantically inside the house?

While some of you might make up a story about attention deficit disorder, early-onset Alzheimer's disease, or just plain stupidity, my story is that I was lost in thought—and that being lost in thought is more than just a metaphor. It's an actual physical reality that many of us experience on a daily basis.

You may be lost in thought right now as you're reading these words. In fact, if you're like most people, you went into your head several times while reading my story, visualizing my dilemma or thinking about times when you or someone you know behaved in a similarly distracted manner.

Although there's nothing wrong with this in theory, in practice, these little mental excursions are filled with detour after detour. By the time we've "come back to our senses," ten minutes have passed and we've forgotten what it was that we went into our heads for in the first place.

In short, we get lost in a morass of our own thoughts and stories—lost to ourselves, lost to our intentions, and lost to the world around us.

And when you're lost in thought, it's virtually impossible to find what you're looking for, whether it's the answer to a question, the next step toward a goal, or a better relationship with the person you're supposedly listening to while you're up in your head, figuring out what to say next.

What's the solution?

Stop driving yourself nuts— and go out of your mind instead.

When we go "out of our minds" and down into our bodies, good things happen. We stop "listening" and actually begin hearing what's being said to us. We stop looking and begin to see what's really going on all around us. As we become more present to our surroundings, we connect more deeply with our feelings. The chatter of the storyteller diminishes and we open up the space to hear the still, small voice of wisdom within.

And when we unplug ourselves from our mental matrix and wake up to the real world, we're finally able to reconnect with our innate happiness, joy, and well-being in the present moment.

Here's one of my favorite exercises that you can use anytime you want to quiet the storyteller and refocus your attention on the task at hand. . . .

The NOW Exercise

1. Count ten breaths from 1 to 10. A simple way to do this is to silently say the word *in* for each inhale and *out* for each exhale. Follow up each word with the number—for example, "In (1), out (1); in (2), out (2)"; and so on.

2. If you lose count before you get to ten (and yes, pretty much everyone does the first few times they do it), simply begin again at one.

3. When you get to ten, smile down into your heart and enjoy the precious present.

I often ask my clients to do this exercise toward the beginning of a session if they seem overwhelmed. They almost never want to do it, yet they nearly always thank me afterward. In fact, the first few times you try it for yourself, you may find it extraordinary how difficult it actually is to get all the way up to ten.

Because it's so easy to drift away into your story while you're reading these words, I've put a little reminder in each of the remaining chapters. Look out for this symbol:

Whenever you see it, check to see if you've become lost in thought. If so, smile down into your body and take the one or two minutes you'll need to do "The NOW Exercise." Each time you do, you're creating an opening for greater happiness to come inside.

Living Without a Story

Byron Katie is a spiritual teacher with a very practical question that she repeatedly asks in many different forms:

Who would you be without your story?

In other words, if you could look behind the curtain of your personal history—your daily log of victories and defeats, betrayals and redemptions, triumphs over adversity, and tragedies over a lifetime—what would you see?

While pondering that question one day, I remembered the following story of a teacher who posed a particularly difficult and frightening dilemma to his favorite student. . . .

"Imagine you are dreaming the most incredibly vivid dream of your life," began the teacher. "In the dream, you seem to be some sort of an adventurer, and each adventure brings with it new challenges and creative solutions. You experience many things—some wonderful and some not so wonderful.

"You soon realize that in your dream, anything is possible. On one of your adventures, you encounter a very high wall, so you imagine yourself a rope and climb to the top. In another, you are falling off a cliff, but before you reach the ground, you begin to fly.

"Eventually, you begin to look forward to each new adventure—until one time, for no apparent reason, everything seems to go wrong.

"It is dark, so dark that you cannot see your hand before your face. Even before you can hear or see anything, you sense danger. Strange and uncomfortable sounds begin crawling out from the depths of your imagination and seem to be coming closer to you.

"Cautiously, you strike a match. Everywhere you look, you're surrounded by the most hideous creatures you've ever seen.

"You try to run, but your legs won't move; you open your mouth to scream, but no sound comes out. Everything you've learned up to this point seems to have abandoned you, and a horrific death seems imminent.

"What would you do?"

The student was lost in thought for many moments, and the teacher could see a range of fearful emotions play across her face as she lived the scenario fully in her mind. Suddenly and without warning, she opened her eyes and began to laugh.

"I know what I would do," the student said. "I would wake up!"

While meditation is traditionally taught as a way of "waking up" from the illusions of the mind, the practice I've found most useful in unraveling my own story and those of my clients is closer to what Tibetan Buddhists call *undistracted nonmeditation:* "undistracted" because you deliberately minimize distractions; "nonmeditation" because you aren't concentrating on anything in particular.

I was first introduced to this idea by my spiritual coach, mentor, and friend Peter Fenner. He calls it "just sitting," and I use it regularly to step outside my story and simply experience life as it is. . . .

The Practice of Nonmeditation

1.   Sit for 20 minutes.

2.   Don't get up.

3.   Don't talk, write, or engage in any other obvious external distractions.

4.   Let your mind go wherever it wants.

There's no way to get this wrong—as long as you remain sitting (you can move about in your seat if you like), you're engaged in the practice.

Even if the stories of your life never go away, they can become less and less of a limiting factor in your quest for happiness and well-being. In the next chapter, we'll look at how your stories can create stress in your life and examine a few of the many choices that will take that stress away. . . .

Chapter Five

<u>STRESS LESS</u>

Angling for Happiness

"If you are distressed by anything external, the pain is not due to the thing itself, but to your estimate of it; and this you have the power to revoke at any moment."
— Marcus Aurelius

When I ask people what causes stress in their lives, they're often quick to come back with a litany of stories about external events ranging from lack of money to problems at work to arguments with loved ones at home.

But, in fact, all stress is caused *internally* by only one thing: resisting reality. Without a story that says things should be other than the way that they are, you couldn't experience any emotional stress.

Think about it—does a stick floating down a river feel stress? No—it flows wherever the water takes it. No story, no stress. How does a plane fly faster and faster through the sky? By adjusting its wing configuration to minimize resistance. Less resistance, more speed (and less stress on the engines and wings).

What makes this "stress as resistance" model so powerful is that once you really get it, you'll see that:

Your experience of stress doesn't come from life pushing on you—it comes from you pushing back!

Now this doesn't mean that resistance is bad. As any weight lifter or bodybuilder will tell you, resistance is an excellent way to develop muscles and build strength. It's just that it's a terrible way to create change.

Change happens easily when you focus on altering what's within your control: your attitude and your actions.

Attitude is one of those unfortunate words that has lost much of its original meaning in the process of becoming a self-help catchphrase. In the field of aeronautics, it refers to the "orientation of an aircraft with respect to the horizon or other frame of reference"—or as my friend John LaValle describes it, the aircraft's "angle of approach."

Used in this sense, it's easy to see how our attitude plays such an important part in lessening the impact of stress in our lives. When we approach the circumstances of our life from certain angles, they can seem overwhelming; when we approach them from a different point of view, we can often overwhelm them.

Each of the "attitude adjustments" that I'll be recommending for reducing your stress and increasing your happiness and well-being corresponds to the steps of Reinhold Niebuhr's famous "Serenity Prayer":

> *"God grant me the serenity to accept*
> *the things I cannot change,*
> *courage to change the things I can,*
> *and the wisdom to know the difference."*

As you learn to stop arguing with reality, let go of trying to control what's outside of your control, and start making clear choices about how you want to be and behave in the world, you'll find yourself with less stress and greater serenity than ever before.

The Three Types of Resistance

There are three main ways that our resistance to life tends to manifest itself as stress in our bodies and minds:

1. Denial
2. Control freaking
3. Choosing not to choose

1. Denial—Arguing That Things Should Not Be as They Are

A seeker journeyed through the furthest regions of the earth to find a teacher rumored to know the secrets of happiness. When he arrived at the teacher's mountaintop retreat, he eagerly awaited his audience with the reclusive man. Finally, his moment came.

"Why have you come?" the teacher asked.

The seeker proceeded to list problem after problem that he was facing in his life.

After listening patiently, the teacher sighed. "I'm afraid I can't help you with your problems."

"Why not?" inquired the puzzled and disappointed seeker.

"Because the gods have decreed that we all must carry 51 problems with us at all times. Even if I could help you solve the problems you tell me of, they would only be replaced with 51 more."

The teacher paused to allow the full significance of the idea to sink in.

"I may, however," he continued, "be able to help you with your 52nd problem."

"What's that?" asked the seeker.

"Your 52nd problem," replied the teacher, "is that you think you shouldn't have the first 51 problems."

We've already discussed the fact that your problems are only problems because of the story that things should be other than the way they are—that either what's happening should *not* be happening, or what isn't happening *should* be happening.

A simple solution is to ask yourself two questions on an ongoing basis:

a. *What's happening right now?* When you ask yourself what's happening right now, it includes what's going on both inside and outside your body and mind.

> So what *is* happening right now? What's taking place that we could all verify if we were watching your life on video? What's happening for you on the inside? What stories are you telling yourself? What pictures, sounds, and feelings are you most aware of now?
>
> How about now?
>
> And now?

The more you ask, the more you'll come into the present moment—a place where there are no problems, only internal experiences and externally verifiable facts.

b. *Could I let go of wanting to change that?* If I had to nominate a single question that would massively reduce your stress and change your life for the better, it would be—somewhat ironically—to ask if you could let go of wanting to change your life for the better and allow things to be exactly as they are . . . for now.

While most people seem to initially resist this question, its magic is that it highlights the ways in which we resist so much of what's happening in our lives. We do this with the best of intentions—after all, we tend to want what's best for ourselves and others. But letting go of *wanting* to change something is different from not changing it, and we don't need to blindly "go with the flow" in order to live a stress-less life. The fact is, intention and desire can peacefully coexist with reality.

Admiral James Stockdale was the highest-ranking United States military officer held in a prisoner-of-war camp during the Vietnam War. For eight years, he was tortured and kept primarily in isolation in a prison with conditions so brutal it became ironically known as the "Hanoi Hilton."

Under these intense and relentless circumstances, Stockdale developed his reputation as a leader, an innovator, and a man with unbreakable character. Many of his fellow POWs credit his influence and example as one of the key factors in their own ability to persevere through otherwise insufferable conditions.

When asked how he managed to stay sane and strong in the face of such brutal conditions, Admiral Stockdale replied: "I never lost faith in the end of the story. I never doubted not only that I would get out, but also that I would prevail in the end and turn the experience into the defining event of my life, which, in retrospect, I would not trade."

When asked who didn't make it out, his answer was considerably more surprising. "The optimists," Stockdale said. "They were the ones who said, 'We're going to be out by Christmas.' And Christmas would come, and Christmas would go. Then they'd say, 'We're going to be out by Easter.' And Easter would come, and Easter would go. And then Thanksgiving, and then it would be Christmas again. And they died of a broken heart."

These seemingly contradictory notions form the basis of what best-selling business author Jim Collins calls the "Stockdale Paradox." In order to succeed in the face of seemingly insurmountable odds, you must:

Retain faith that you will prevail in the end,
regardless of the difficulties.

And at the same time:

> *Confront the most brutal facts of your current reality,*
> *whatever they might be.*

It's not hope that hurts, but expectation. "Expecting" something that's outside your control is a recipe for suffering. Yet hope—the belief in the possibility that tomorrow can be better than today—carries with it the energy and inspiration to make it so.

In the words of Winston Churchill:

> *"If you're going through hell, be sure to keep going."*

Choosing Faith

1. Think of a situation you're currently facing that feels almost too much for you to handle.

2. Create an inventory of all the relevant details of your current reality. Be sure to stick to the facts, making things neither better nor worse than you find them.

3. If you knew that everything was going to turn out right in the end, what would you be inspired to do today to reach your goals?

2. Control Freaking—Trying to Control What's Outside Your Control

In one of the first self-help books ever written (around 2,000 years ago), the Stoic philosopher Epictetus began his *Enchiridion* with these words:

> Happiness and freedom begin with a clear understanding of one principle: Some things are within our control, and some things are not.

Yet if you've gotten out of bed this morning, it's a safe bet that you've already tried to control at least a few dozen things you can't control—even if you're reading this book just after breakfast.

Notice how many of these things you tried to exert some control over in the past 24 hours:

- What your partner or children said or did

- The behavior of other drivers or commuters on the way to work

- A co-worker's opinion of you

- How something you've already done works out

While reporting on rowing at the 1996 Olympics, sports broadcaster Charlie Jones interviewed a number of the competing athletes. Anytime he asked them a question about something that was outside their control (such as the weather, the strengths and weaknesses of their opponents, or what might go wrong during a race), the Olympians would respond with the phrase "that's outside my boat."

By refusing to focus on anything that was beyond their control, these athletic champions were able to bring all their resources to bear on what was within their control—everything from their physiology, mental maps, and stories to the actions that they took preparing for and competing in the actual event.

In my own life, I've found that focusing exclusively on what's "inside my boat" not only increases my effectiveness, but often eliminates stress altogether.

Here's a simple way to put this strategy into action:

The Serenity Record

1. As you go about your day today, stick a little note on the inside cover of this book or in your pocket. Draw a line down the middle of the paper.

2. Every time you exert effort or direct a thought toward something you can't control, make a small mark on the left side of the line; each time you focus on what's within your control or use the power you have to change something for the better, make a mark on the right side of the line.

3. At the end of the day, review your "serenity record." What did you learn about yourself? About your work and life? About what you can control and what you can't?

---

3. Choosing Not to Choose—
How to Be a Victim of Circumstance

A third type of stress in life is the result of feeling as if you have no choice about something. As soon as you recognize the decisions that are inherent in any situation, you'll regain a sense of being in control—and the stressful feelings will begin to disappear. The more you focus on these choices, the greater the sense of well-being and control you will experience.

Here are three types of choices you can always make, regardless of what's happening around you:

a. Choosing how to be On paper, I had a very happy childhood. I was loved, I grew up in a nice home, and whatever things my parents may have found difficult to deal with in their lives were handled in a manner that kept us away from any sense of external stress. Yet I was miserable, depressed, and even suicidal for large periods of that time.

My best friend had a more difficult childhood. His parents divorced when he was very young, and his older brother was killed in a car crash when he was 15. He lived in a double-wide trailer, and the money that had been put aside to send him to college had disappeared into the monthly expenses years before he was able to use it. Yet he was happy, positive, and cheerful throughout.

At the time, I didn't know that how I chose to be was up to me; consequently, I felt like a victim of my moods. My friend didn't know about the power to choose, but his "default" was simply inclined toward the positive. Now we're both aware of the power within us—and while we don't always choose to be happy, peaceful, accepting, and kind, we do so enough of the time to take most of what life throws at us in stride. (And on occasion, to throw back the stuff we don't want to keep!)

b. Choosing how to see Unlike road maps, which must accurately reflect the territory they describe in order to be useful, our mental maps actually re-create the territory as they're describing it. Since these maps often become self-fulfilling prophecies, we can change our experience of the world (and ultimately the world itself) by changing the way we choose to see it.

In other words:

Over time, the map becomes the territory.

The way you choose to see your life will have a dramatic impact on the way your life turns out to be. If you see the world as a friendly place, you'll tend to notice the ways in which situations work out for the best. Because you're looking for "friendly" things to happen, you're that much more likely to find them. At times, you may even create them with your intention and actions.

Here are just a few of the "ways of seeing" that are available to us at any moment:

- Friendly or unfriendly
- Good or evil
- Malicious or well intended
- By design or at random
- Mean-spirited or frightened
- Stupid or misinformed

c. Choosing what to do (or not do) An actress client once called me in a dither, claiming she was "stressed to the eyeballs" because she was being bossed around on the set by a famously belligerent director. I asked her why she was putting up with it, and she said, "I have no choice—he's the director!"

I told her the following story:

One day, Zeus was sitting atop Mount Olympus when he saw a beautiful doe being chased by an angry stag. The doe was heading to the sanctuary of the forest, but the king of all the gods could see that the stag was too close behind her. He immediately thought to cast a lightning bolt through the heart of the stag, but decided to wait and see how the drama would play out.

A few moments later, the stag stopped suddenly and turned away from the doe. Zeus caught sight of a huge gray wolf charging into view at full speed. The wolf and stag battled for what seemed like hours until finally the wolf slunk away, defeated.

Immediately the doe came to the side of the stag, nuzzling his wounds and gently guiding him on toward the safety of the forest.

I then suggested to the actress that she make the following three choices:

1. How she wanted to be in relation to the situation at work: that is, her physiological state

2. How she wanted to "see" the situation: that is, her angle of approach

3. What (if anything) she wanted to do

The following week, she called to tell me that she had first chosen to be centered and strong on the set the next day. In order to do that, she used some of the same tools I've shared with you in this book. She had then chosen to see the director as "scared" instead of "angry."

By making these choices, she felt able to neither fight back nor withdraw when he confronted her. Instead, she simply listened to him with her full attention and then did as he asked. At the end of the day, the director came up to her and apologized for his behavior—something that a nearby crew member claimed he'd never seen happen before.

Here's a quick experiment you can do anytime you're feeling like a victim of your own life:

1. Think of a situation you've been finding stressful. If you knew it was up to you, how would you choose to be in relation to that situation today?

2. On a piece of paper, make a list of all the ways this situation is "bad for you." Now turn the paper over and make a list of at least as many

ways in which the situation could be seen as "good for you." Take a look at each side of the paper in turn and notice how you feel. Whose side are you going to take? Which way are you going to choose to see the situation?

3. When you've decided how you want to be in yourself and how you want to see the situation, choose whether or not to take action at this time. If you decide to take action, do it within the next 24 hours if at all possible.

Of course, when you're in the midst of anxiety, overwhelming emotions, or even panic, it can be difficult to remember that you always have a choice. That's why in our next chapter together, we'll explore some additional ways of mastering our response to what happens when our lives seem to be spinning out of control. . . .

Chapter Six

<u>OVERCOMING ANXIETY</u>

Four Magic Words for a Balanced Life

> *"Words were originally magic, and to this day words have
> retained much of their ancient magical power."*
> — Sigmund Freud

One of the things that has always impressed me about my wife is her equanimity—her ability to treat life's ups and downs with relative calm, becoming neither a diva when times are good nor an ogre when times are hard. When I asked her the secret to her authentically peaceful demeanor, she told me that whenever she felt herself cruising out of control—soaring too high or flying too low—she repeated four simple words that always brought her back to center.

To my amazement, they were the same four words that I'd first read in a story many years earlier about the secret to stepping off life's roller coaster. The story goes something like this. . . .

Once upon a time, there was a great king who recognized that the more powerful he became, the more important it was to avoid the kind of impulsive action that can accompany both life's highs and life's lows. He tasked his council of wisdom to devise some means of reminding him that his best self lay in the middle path between laughter and tears, joy and sorrow, high and low.

Soon they returned to him with a red-jeweled ring. Inscribed beneath the stone, the wise counselors told him, was a magical incantation. If the king became drunk with the giddiness of success, it would sober him up and enable him to remain wise; if he was lost in the hopelessness of despair, it would bring him faith and courage.

Before the king had a chance to look beneath the stone and read the incantation, he found himself transported as if by magic to a room filled with the sound of the most beautiful voices he had ever heard. The king was quickly hypnotized by the voices' siren call and began to follow wherever they led.

Just as the enchanting voices were about to lead him over the edge of a cliff, the jewel on his ring began to glow; and in its light, he read for the first time the magical incantation:

This too will pass.

Instantly, the king regained his senses, saw the voices for what they were, and turned his back on them. But no sooner had he done so than he found himself once again magically transported. This time he was trapped on a battlefield, his men lying dead or wounded, his kingdom all but lost. A lone rider was charging toward him, sword drawn. Just as the king was about to resign himself to his fate, the jewel on his ring once more began to glow, and he again read the incantation:

This too will pass.

Suddenly emboldened by hope, the king found a new strength and knocked the rider from his mount. Rallying his remaining troops, he turned the tide of the battle, saving the kingdom and all who dwelled within.

Like the king, you have the power within you to balance your perceptions and live free from your fantasies and nightmares. But you'll need to find your own way to access that power—and you can only ever do that right here, right now.

Finding the Moment

I was feeling out of sorts and a bit run down one rainy day recently, so I drove over to see my local doctor. She looked at me and asked what I thought was a very unusual question: "Are you having a really good week?"

As I had just closed several large deals—which meant, in theory, I could pretty much take the rest of the year off—I replied, "Yes, I suppose I am."

"I thought so," she said. "I've never seen you this stressed."

What was interesting about that exchange was that it hadn't occurred to me that I could get just as worked up about things going well in my life as I could about things going poorly.

When I looked at the elements common to both scenarios, the connection became clear: Whether things seemed to be going extremely poorly or extremely well, my focus was on the future, not the moment. And the future (over which we have no direct control) can be a very anxious place in which to live. The only moment we have any real control over is this one . . . and of course, this one right now.

As I drove home in the rain, lost in thought, I heard the unmistakable sound of a car skidding toward me across the road. I snapped out of my thought trance, slammed on my own brakes, and mercifully, everyone was completely fine.

Better still, I had found the moment (you know, this one)—and in just a few moments, all the anxiety I'd been experiencing dissipated and was replaced by a gentle "background bliss."

Since then, I've been fairly grounded in the present (it's happening right now) and have reaped the benefits of relatively stress-free living (despite each of my children coming down with the flu in the space of the last 72 hours).

But as I sat down to write today, it occurred to me that narrowly avoiding a car accident—useful though it was for me in finding the moment (are you here yet?)—wasn't a terribly practical experiment to suggest to others. So instead, I've filled this chapter with some of my favorite ways to find the moment, overcome anxiety, and live out beyond the edge of fear.

Spinning Your Fears

> *"Let the great world spin forever down the ringing grooves of change."*
> — Alfred, Lord Tennyson

Our nervous systems are conditioned to create stability but to notice change. This is a part of our tremendous adaptability as human beings and frees up our conscious attention to be able to notice difference.

As a part of his ongoing innovation in the art and science of personal change, Dr. Richard Bandler has developed a simple technique called "spinning," which makes use of this natural functioning of the nervous system to reduce bad feelings and amplify good ones.

Here's an abbreviated transcript of how I used it with a caller on my radio show who wanted to feel less anxiety and more happiness in her life:

Me: Where do you feel anxiety in your body?

Caller: Everywhere, I guess. I just feel scared, and I don't know what I'm scared of.

Me: I'm not so worried about what you're scared of—do you feel any fear in your body right now?

C: No, not right now.

Me: Could you scare yourself just a little bit? Go on, think about the future . . . can you bring up just a little bit of fear right now?

C: Yes.

Me: Where in your body does it start—where are you first aware of it?

C: I think in my head.

Me: And where does it go?

C: Down my back.

Me: Great. Now in order for you to continue experiencing the feeling, it has to keep moving. So if it starts in your head and goes down your back, where does it go next? Back up to the top of your head?

C: It comes back to my chest.

Me: Okay, and does it spin toward you or away from you?

C: Toward me.

Me: Toward you—great. Now here's what I'm going to ask you to do: I want you to imagine that you're pulling the spinning fear out of your body so you can see it in front of you. You can see it spinning toward you, but it's all happening in front of your body right now.

C: Okay.

Me: Now, I want you to turn it upside down so now it's spinning the other way—it's spinning away from you.

C: Right.

Me: What's your favorite color?

C: Um . . . pink.

Me: Okay, I want you to make it pink. So it's pink and it's spinning away from you and I want you to put it right back inside your body. Bring it back inside your body so you can feel it spinning down through your chest and up your back, up to the top of your head and back down your chest and it's spinning away from you and it's a lovely pink color. How does that feel?

C: *(surprised and laughing a bit)* It feels great!

Me: Okay, so now I want you to spin it faster and faster . . . how does it feel the faster you spin it?

C: *(with great sincerity)* It feels great. . . .

Me: And I want you to take that great feeling and let it spread from the top of your head down to the tips of your toes, right out to the edges of your fingertips, and the more you spin the feeling, the easier it will be for you to have this feeling anytime you want just by taking control of it—because it's not just a feeling, it's *your* feeling. . . .

There are so many theories about "why we feel this" or "why we feel that," but sometimes if what we want to do is feel better, the simplest thing to do is just step right back into your body and take control.

Here's how you can begin to play with this technique for yourself:

Be Your Own "Spin Doctor"

1. Think about something that makes you feel angry, sad, or fearful.

2. Observe where in your body the feeling starts. Where's the very first place that you're aware of feeling that way?

3. Now, notice where the feeling moves to next. Does it go up, down, left, right, or in some other direction? (In order for you to feel a feeling, it must be moving; otherwise, the nerves habituate and you won't feel them any more!)

4. When you've identified where the feeling begins and where it moves to, notice which direction it's spinning in. If it doesn't feel as though it's spinning, ask yourself which way it would be spinning if it were. This could be toward you or away from you on a vertical, horizontal, or even diagonal plane.

---

5. Next, imagine pulling the feeling out of your body so it continues to spin in front of you. Turn it upside down so that it's now spinning in the opposite direction. If you like, imagine it being your favorite color.

6. Now pull the "new and improved" feeling back into your body, continuing to spin it in the new direction. The faster you spin it, the better it will feel.

7. Anytime you begin to feel the old feeling, you can simply reverse the direction of the spin and take control!

You can use this same technique to amplify a good feeling. Simply notice the direction of the spin, add some color, make it bigger, and spin it faster.

When Panic Attacks

When I first learned NLP, I worked in a more directly therapeutic role than I do now. For whatever reason, I wound up seeing a lot of clients who experienced "panic attacks." The structure of a panic attack is a curious thing. In nearly every case I came across, there was a defining incident—a time when specific things had been truly painful, and the person felt out of control.

The actual panic attacks, however, came anytime the person felt what he or she believed to be the *onset* of another "out of control" experience. In other words, what created the panic was the attempt to prevent it from happening. It was actually the fear of fear—panicking now about the possibility of panicking in the future.

I remember one particular client who came to me with such bad panic attacks that she arrived at my office lying on the backseat of her boyfriend's car with a coat draped over her head. I asked her to come in, gave her a cup of tea, and then told her that I was taking a poll and needed to know the answer to a very important question: What are the two silliest words in the English language?

After a bit of confusion and some curious thought, she came up with the words *french fry* and *parka*. When it came time to take her case history, I asked her to tell me all about her problem with one caveat: Instead of the phrase "panic attack," which I explained was much too scary a term for me, she was to substitute the word *french fry*. And rather than telling me about the out-of-control feeling, would she mind substituting the word *parka?*

We then had a fascinating, fun, and funny time discussing how many times a week she had "french fries," what it was about "french fries" that she found most scary. Eventually, I had her tell me about her first "french fry."

In addition, she talked about that horrible "parka" feeling and how whenever she felt herself starting to "parka," she'd immediately begin having a "french fry."

Sometimes when I tell this story, people think I was being disrespectful, but consider this: For two years, this woman had been unable to leave her apartment without a coat over her head, and within ten minutes, she was laughing about it. She was beginning to access her own good feelings in relation to the problem situation—and those good feelings would be the key to her finding her own solutions.

Here's an exercise you can do to notice the incredible difference that introducing good feelings into "bad" situations can make. Be kind to yourself by doing it with something that's only a little bit uncomfortable until you get the hang of it. If you're dealing with something really traumatic, I recommend you only do this with a qualified (and open-minded!) helping professional.

Mickey Mouse Therapy

1. Choose something you'd like to feel better about in your life. On a scale from 1 to 10, where 1 is awful/terrible/helpless and 10 is wonderful and completely resourceful, how do you feel in relation to it?

2. Talk out loud about it for at least three minutes in a high, squeaky "Mickey Mouse" voice. Be sure to really go for it—"slightly squeaky" won't do the trick.

    If you feel silly talking in a Mickey Mouse voice, try hopping on one leg instead. If that still seems too silly for something as serious as your problem, talk in the Mickey Mouse voice while hopping on one leg!

3. Notice what's different when you think about the situation now. How do you feel about it on a scale from 1 to 10?

What You're Really Afraid of . . .

"All fear is the fear that unhappiness will happen."
— Bruce Di Marsico

I used to be deathly afraid of three things: investing, heights, and commitment (to anything!). When I began to consider the radical idea that we aren't so much afraid of what might happen to us as of how we think we'll feel about what will happen to us, I looked more deeply at what had at first seemed straightforward.

When I first went inside and listened to my fearful thoughts, it became apparent that I was afraid of investing because I thought I might lose all my money and have to beg on the streets. I was afraid of heights because I thought I might lose control and jump. I was afraid of commitment because I thought I might miss out on something better that came along later.

Yet as I listened more closely to my inner stories, I realized that what I was really afraid of was the potential embarrassment and humiliation of losing all my money and winding up on the streets. I was frightened of all the pain I'd cause my loved ones if I lost control, and I was terrified that if I made a commitment and then something seemingly better came along, I'd feel stupid and kick myself for the rest of my life.

The moment I realized that what I was really afraid of was my own feelings of unhappiness, I knew exactly what to do. Here's how it works:

The more you're willing to feel good about whatever it is that you're feeling, the happier you get to feel. The more conditions you put on your good feelings and happiness, the fewer good feelings you get to feel. The choice, as always, is yours.

Feeling Good about Feeling Bad

1. Tune in to how you're feeling in your body right now.

2. Whatever it is that you're feeling, could you love or appreciate the feeling exactly as it is?

3. If not, could you love or appreciate yourself for feeling the feeling?

4. If not, could you love or appreciate yourself for *not* being willing or able to love or appreciate yourself for feeling the feeling?

5. Continue on "up the ladder" of perception until you're feeling a genuine sense of love or appreciation for some aspect of whatever you're experiencing now.

Know Fear

> *"Fear is a habit; I am not afraid."*
> — Aung San Suu Kyi, winner of the
> 1991 Nobel Prize for Peace

Having explored the fear of unhappiness for many years now, I've come to realize that while we can reduce our fear with techniques, dispute it with our minds, and confront it with our actions, there's a simpler and much more difficult point of view:

**99.9 percent of fear isn't really fear—
it's superstition.**

We've been taught since we were little children that fear is necessary to keep us safe and motivate us to move forward. In fact, it's a poor substitute for knowledge, intuition, and inspiration.

Knowledge of what would happen if we were hit by a car is more than enough to get most of us to look both ways before we cross the street, even if we no longer hear our parents' voices ringing in our ears to "Stay back!" Our intuitive awareness of danger will let us know not to trust the smiling stranger even while our love/hate relationship with fear tries to confuse the issue. And the inspiration to live a life we love will carry us forward long after the adrenaline burst from fearing a life we hate has burned out.

Knowing this doesn't mean you won't ever feel fear again—old conditioning tends not to disappear overnight. It just means that you don't have to be afraid.

I invite you to use whatever's going on in your life right now to begin a "fear-less" experiment:

For the next few days (or weeks or even months), choose to live as if fear is completely unnecessary. When you're about to do something, ask yourself whether or not it's coming from fear. If it's from fear, don't do it. If you're not sure what to do, ask yourself what you would do if you weren't afraid—and do that.

Be kind to yourself along the way—the fear-less path isn't always an easy one to travel, especially at first. But after you've been on it for a while, it's difficult to go back to living the other kind of life.

Chapter Seven

BEHAVIORAL PROZAC™

The Art of Staying "Whelmed"

Main Entry: de·pres·sion
Pronunciation: di-'prə-shen, dē-
Function: noun
Date: 14th century

(1): a state of feeling sad : DEJECTION (2): a psychoneurotic or psychotic disorder marked especially by sadness, inactivity, difficulty in thinking and concentration, a significant increase or decrease in appetite and time spent sleeping, feelings of dejection and hopelessness, and sometimes suicidal tendencies (1): a reduction in activity, amount, quality, or force (2): a lowering of vitality or functional activity

Or, to put it more succinctly, being in a really, really bad mood and feeling that you can't do anything about it and wouldn't want to if you could . . .

When I worked in television in the U.K., my nickname was "Crazy Mike" because I was pretty much the only one in the cast or crew *not* on antidepressant medication. This wasn't because I was opposed in theory to the use of medication (or herbal treatments) to help regulate brain chemistry, but because I had genuinely found that the techniques I'm sharing with you in this book produced a similarly positive effect on my mind and body.

So while I'll give you some specific ideas and techniques in this chapter that I've found useful in dealing with depression both personally and professionally, everything you've learned up to this point still counts:

1. You can feel good (or at least feel better) in any moment by going to your heart, focusing on "happy" or loving thoughts, imagining good feelings spreading throughout your body, and then focusing on the benefits of feeling good both now and in the future.

2. You can reduce your bad feelings by changing your story, turning down the volume on the storyteller, and taking ten slow and gentle breaths.

3. You can relieve your stress by letting go of what's outside your control (and taking hold of what's within it), loving what is, and choosing how you want to be in relation to the events of your life.

4. You can release anxiety and feel better in any moment by spinning it backward and choosing to see things from a different perspective.

Yet so often what paralyzes people suffering from depression is the sense that there's no point in doing anything (and no energy to do it, even if there was a point). Psychologists call this phenomenon "learned helplessness"—a state of mind where individuals have "learned" (or convinced themselves) that nothing they do will make any difference to the outcome of a situation.

What makes the research in learned helplessness so encouraging is the discovery that happiness, optimism, and the related positive states and actions can also be learned. By taking small, seemingly insignificant "baby steps" in the direction of your goals and dreams, you can quickly create changes that not only lessen the symptoms of depression but can also bring more energy, hope, and vitality into your daily life.

What I want to share with you specifically in the rest of this chapter are ten small changes you can make in your thinking and doing that will create a tremendous difference to your feelings of happiness, vitality, and well-being.

Consider them an unofficial prescription for "Behavioral Prozac™." . . .

1. Be unhappy. I remember a friend of my wife's coming up to me at a party and, with the same cheery smile she always seemed to wear, asking me if I thought she needed to seek medical treatment for depression.

After pointing out that I wasn't a doctor and, therefore, not qualified to dole out anything resembling medical advice, I nonetheless asked her to tell me if there was anything going on in her life that she thought might be behind her depressed feelings.

"Well," she told me, "my dad was just diagnosed with cancer—do you think that might have anything to do with it?"

"Hmm . . ." I responded, trying hard to stifle an embarrassed smile. "Is there anything else?"

She thought for a moment, and then said, "My fiancé left me. We'd been going out for 13 years, and he finally proposed on my 30th birthday. Then about six months into the engagement, he told me he was leaving me for his secretary, whom he'd been having an affair with and who was now pregnant."

At this point, I'm ashamed to admit that I burst out laughing. When she began to protest, I apologized and told her that I didn't think she needed to seek medical treatment for depression—she simply needed to allow herself to feel angry and sad.

One of the oddest things I've learned in my own quest for happiness is that the easiest way to change a feeling is to take the time to actually feel it. That's not to say you need to suffer—most feelings transform pretty quickly once they've been felt. But the more you push them down in an attempt not to feel them, the more "depressed" you begin to feel.

Feeling my feelings is neither expressing nor repressing. It's simply acknowledging that I'm experiencing them right here, right now. Rather than distracting myself from my discomfort or trying to "fix" my sadness, anger, or fear, I close my eyes and focus directly on the feeling in my body. As I go deeper into the feeling, I find to my amazement that within as little as 30 seconds, the stuck feeling begins to dissolve into a gentle flow of endorphins.

This simple trick brings with it an incredible gift— when you feel your feelings instead of fearing them, you reconnect to your body's natural wisdom and experience new levels of guidance, freedom, and joy.

PRESCRIPTION 1: Feeling Your Feelings

Take some time now to feel into your body. Don't worry about labeling what you feel and don't do anything to try and change it—just tune in and feel what you feel. Stick with it until you notice the feelings begin to change for the better.

---

2. Move your body. There is extensive research on the positive effects of exercise on mood. In fact, Dr. Michael J. Norden, the author of *Beyond Prozac,* has been quoted as saying: "Ninety minutes on a treadmill doubles brain serotonin levels." The problem is that when you're in the throes of depression, the chances of your spending 90 minutes on a treadmill are pretty low. Still, if you think of exercise as both a preventive method and a tonic, it can form an important part of your Behavioral Prozac™ prescription.

Joseph Campbell once described money as "congealed energy," and the same can be said about a static physical body. When you move your body, your energy begins to flow again; and as your body comes alive, it becomes easier and easier to stay tuned in to it.

If nothing else, moving your body forces you to pay attention to it, at least for a few moments. And when you drop your attention back down into your body, you might find yourself getting all the way back into your life.

PRESCRIPTION 2: Move It and Lose It

Move your body for at least 30 seconds. It doesn't matter if you don't feel like it—just flap your arms, move your legs, and get into action! If you're in a room where you can get away with it, make some noise—scream, sing, shout, or blather like an idiot!

Now . . .

Close your eyes and tune in to the sensations happening in your body right now. When you're ready, open your eyes and move back into your daily activity while continuing to be aware of this simple feeling of being in your body.

3. Put yourself first—at least for now. Whenever my clients begin telling me how difficult they've been finding their life, the first question I ask is: "What have you been doing for self-care this week?" Invariably, they get a sheepish look on their face and mutter something about having been "really busy."

But not taking excellent care of yourself is more often the cause of overwhelm than its effect. When we feel cared for in ourselves (because we've taken the time to do those things that we know really make a difference to our happiness and well-being), we're generally capable of far more than life sends our way.

Perhaps the most difficult yet rewarding place to practice taking excellent care of yourself is in your relationships. The typical cycle in a relationship goes something like this:

- *I give in to some request that I don't really want to go along with in order to be nice and/or avoid conflict.*

- *I then become angry and resentful as I replay the incident in my mind over and over again—each review becoming slightly more skewed toward portraying myself as the victim and my loved one as the perpetrator.*

- *I then seek to punish them by sulking, being sarcastic, or denying something that he or she wants.*

Think about it for yourself:

Identify an incident in your personal life that you're angry or upset about. . . .

- Where did you put someone else's needs ahead of your own in relation to that incident?

- How are you now attempting to "get back at them" for "what they did to you"?

(Hint: The term *passive aggressive* is usually relevant here.)

We can break that cycle at any moment by putting our relationship with ourselves before our relationship with others. We only prioritize our partner's or children's wants over our own in those moments when we honestly recognize that it's at least as much fun to be loving as to be loved, and when we've done whatever we need to do for ourselves that allows us to be fully present with others.

If the idea of putting yourself first still seems uncomfortable or inappropriate, consider that it's nearly impossible to be genuinely considerate of others until we've first considered what we need to be happy in ourselves. In the words of Dr. Marshall B. Rosenberg, the founder of The Center for Nonviolent Communication:

> Please don't give me anything or do anything for me unless you can do so with the kind of joy a little child has when it feeds a hungry duck.

PRESCRIPTION 3: Meet Your Own Needs

1. Jot down at least three simple things someone could do to make you feel loved and cared for. For example:

    - Bring me a cup of tea and a cookie.
    - Rub my shoulders.
    - Tell me that they love me.

2. Do each one of those things for yourself as soon as possible. If that feels weird and uncomfortable, feel the discomfort and do it anyway!

3. Put your hands on your heart, close your eyes, and tune in to your body. Ask yourself, *What can I do to take better care of myself right now?*

4. Do it!

4. Connect with people you love and care about. I have a friend who has been successfully involved with a 12-step program for many years. I once asked him if he felt that he still needed the program to stay sober. His reply stuck with me: "Even if I don't, getting together on a regular basis with a group of friends to share my problems and victories in an atmosphere of unconditional love strikes me as a pretty great way to spend my free time."

There's a tremendous urge to isolate yourself when you're feeling particularly down, yet research in the field of neurotheology has shown that a sense of peace and well-being invariably follows the shift from a "me" focus to a "we" focus. Whether you find that connection most easily with family, friends, God, or nature, connecting with something larger than yourself is a reliable way of ensuring that your heart stays open and your life stays sweet—in short, a pretty great way to spend your free time!

PRESCRIPTION 4: Make Someone's Day

Just for today, make whomever you're with the most important person in the world. Turn off your cell phone in the middle of the day. Astonish a stranger with kindness. Send flowers to an old friend or a love letter to your partner. Offer to pick up lunch at the office or buy coffee for strangers at Starbucks.

Wherever you are and whomever you are with, ask yourself, *What could I do to make this person's day?*

---

5. Breathe deeply. Any emotion that you're experiencing in your body is connected to a specific pattern of breathing. Change your breathing (by slowing it down, speeding it up, inhaling more deeply into your stomach, or even more shallowly into your chest) and you'll transform the way you feel.

One breathing exercise my clients and I find particularly useful for changing the way you feel about a specific situation in your life comes from the work of Dr. Win Wenger:

PRESCRIPTION 5: Relief Breathing

1. Think of a situation in your life that has been getting you down.

2. Imagine wearing a hot, heavy, clammy suit of armor. Feel it begin to weigh you down, compressing and constricting your body.

3. Now imagine removing the armor, and enjoy breathing a huge sigh of relief.

4. For the next minute, breathe as if each inhale is your first breath free of the burdensome weight of the armor.

5. Check back in with your situation. Chances are, it no longer feels like such a burden. You may even find yourself with new insights and a renewed sense of energy and vigor.

---

6. Stop breathing (but only for a moment). One of my favorite quotes, for which I've never satisfactorily found an author, is:

"Life isn't measured by the number of breaths you take, but by the moments which take your breath away."

In the past week, I've had my breath taken away by:

- Hearing my four-year-old daughter's giggle when I tucked her in for the night

- Listening to my nine-year-old daughter singing along to *High School Musical*

- Watching my 12-year-old son dancing when he thought I wasn't looking

- Gazing at my wife coming down the stairs dressed to the nines for an evening out

- Seeing my dogs cuddled up with one another sound asleep on the sofa

- The view out over the valley on a midnight hike with a friend

- A scene in a movie about a family who lived in a lighthouse

Each time your breath is taken away by the beauty of nature, love, or even a sappy, happy movie, you're born again into that moment—and by taking the time to collect those moments, you get to relive them whenever you choose.

While I'm not advocating getting all your medical advice from Julie Andrews, you could do worse than make a list of a few of your favorite things . . . you may find that suddenly you feel glad.

PRESCRIPTION 6: A Few of My Favorite Things

Make a list of all the things you can think of that "make" you happy, from the sound of a cat purring to the taste of your favorite food. Carry the list with you at all times and add to it whenever you can.

Anytime you're feeling a bit down and in need of a pick-me-up, read through your list until you begin to feel an inner smile. Let that smile flow through your whole body until you're once again feeling good on the inside.

---

7. Give yourself something to look forward to. While it's difficult to play chicken and egg with your moods (Are you mad at the chicken because you're in a bad mood, or are you in a bad mood because the chicken's not laying enough eggs?), one consistent element in most people's depression is a sense of hopelessness and futility.

Holding a positive vision of the future becomes easy when you take the emphasis off "positive thinking" (which is pretty near impossible when you're depressed anyway) and focus instead on giving yourself something to look forward to on a daily basis.

PRESCRIPTION 7: It's a Wonderful Life

Take out your daily planner or calendar and put in at least one activity for each of the next 30 days that you'll really look forward to doing. These don't have to cost money, although it's okay if they do. Plan a walk in the park, lunch with a friend, a trip to the movies, or a visit to a museum—anything that brings a smile to your face and a warm feeling to your heart when you think about it.

If you're having trouble with this, enlist the help of a creative and optimistic friend!

---

8. Externalize your inner dialogue. One of the often overlooked similarities between keeping a diary and many of the popular "talk therapies," which have been in vogue since the turn of the last century, is the fact that they get you to voice your secret stories.

A funny thing happens when you externalize your inner dialogue: As you tune in to yourself and become more aware of what you're thinking, you tend to think less and find nicer things to say.

Think about it—do you gossip more to someone's face or behind their back? (Well, not you, but perhaps some of your less-enlightened friends. . . .)

The same thing is true within us—we'll invariably be kinder to ourselves when we write or speak our truth aloud than when we silently criticize ourselves in the supposed privacy of our own minds.

PRESCRIPTION 8: A Conversation Between Friends

Take a piece of paper and make two columns. Write your inner dialogue in one column and your response to that dialogue in the other.

If the comments in the first column are helpful, kind, or contribute to your happiness in any way, acknowledge that in the second column with a simple "Thank you."

In the event that your storyteller is not contributing useful or kind thoughts, use the second column to counter those thoughts with some that make you feel better, cause you to laugh out loud, or simply offer compassion for how you're feeling now.

---

9. Have an ordinary day. Research into teenage suicide has revealed that many of the problems kids have in coping with the realities of daily life stem from the fantasies that adults feed them (and themselves) about how wonderfully perfect our lives are supposed to be.

When you're feeling less than your best, adjust your expectations. Stop trying to have such an extraordinary life for a little while, and allow yourself to have a wonderfully ordinary one instead.

PRESCRIPTION 9: What Do You Expect?

The next time you find yourself fantasizing about how perfect your life is supposed to be (or lamenting over how wonderfully perfect it *isn't*), take whatever you're expecting to the extreme until you can't help but smile:

If you're expecting to have a bad day, imagine what it would be like to have the worst day in the history of bad days—every negative thing you're expecting comes to pass and your car breaks down and it starts to rain a plague of frogs (but only on you).

If you think things are going to be absolutely amazing, notice what happens if everything good you already expect comes to pass and you win the lottery and the Swedish volleyball team's bus breaks down outside your home.

By visiting the polar extremes of expectation, you may be surprised to find out how much fun there is to be had in the wide-open spaces between your worst nightmares and your wildest dreams. . . .

10. Die a little. In the book *Toxic Success,* Dr. Paul Pearsall quotes a woman with cancer who was reflecting on what she had learned:

When you're dying, you really pay attention to your family, to the trees, to the smell of a hot cup of coffee. . . . I drank coffee every morning of my life and never enjoyed the smell as much as I do now. When you face death, you realize you could have been paying attention to all these things and millions more like them every day if you had only put your mind to it. If you want a definition of success, mine is short and sweet: Wake up and smell the coffee.

When you wake up each morning and remember that you're lucky to be alive, it becomes easier to "not sweat the small stuff." And when you stop taking your life for granted, you come to realize that the small stuff is usually the good stuff. In the words of the architect Ludwig Mies van der Rohe, "God is in the details."

PRESCRIPTION 10: Wake Up and Smell the Coffee

There are two ways to do this exercise:

1. Imagine that today is your last day on Earth. Notice how your focus changes, and pay special attention to the things that matter most to you. Many people describe this as bringing a sense of the sacred to their everyday routine.

2. Imagine that today is your first day on Earth. Don't declare yourself to the natives just yet— simply observe, absorb, and enjoy the many bizarre and wonderful things this planet has to offer throughout the day.

One Final Prescription for Behavioral Prozac™ . . .

1. What are some of the things you tend to do when you have a good day—things that nurture your spirit and "make" you feel good? For example:

   - Going out for coffee with friends
   - Writing in your diary
   - Meditating
   - Taking a walk in nature

2. What are some of the ways you traditionally mess yourself up or bring yourself down? For example:

   - Arguing over nothing with your loved ones

   - Trying to get too much done

   - Eating sweets

   - Watching the news before bed

3. What are some quotes or sayings that uplift and inspire you?

Based on the ideas in this chapter and your answers to these questions, create your own prescription for Behavioral Prozac™. Take a piece of paper and put an inspirational quotation right up at the top, and then jot down a list of three to seven things you can do daily to ensure that you have the best possible chance of making it a great day. Keep it as simple as possible, but no simpler—you can always adapt it as you go.

Here's an example of how it might look:

**Prescription for Alex Johnson
for Behavioral Prozac™**

*"The idea that suffering is an illusion
negates compassion; the idea that
it is real negates wisdom."*
— Peter Fenner

Today, I will . . .

. . . *go for a 30-minute walk*

. . . *read from an inspirational book*

. . . *limit my to-do list to five items
(and make sure I do them!)*

. . . *drink eight glasses of water*

. . . *give myself something to look
forward to*

. . . *write at least a page in my diary*

You can use the form on the following page to write your own personalized prescription for Behavioral Prozac™. (If you'd like me to send you some blank "prescription" forms with a range of inspirational quotes, send an e-mail to behavioralprozac@geniuscatalyst.com.)

Prescription for _____
for Behavioral Prozac™

Today, I will . . .

Of course, one of the biggest mistakes people make when they're on medication for their moods is to assume that on days when they feel well, they no longer need to take their meds. Although they may get away with it for a day or two, invariably the original condition returns, often stronger than before.

The antidote is simple:

The more often you take your Behavioral Prozac™ on good days, the more good days you will have.

A Sacred Journey to Happiness

*"Beyond all ideas of wrongdoing and rightdoing,
there is a field. I'll meet you there."*
— Rumi

In Buddhism, the unconditioned mind is sometimes described as "the ultimate medicine"—a place beyond pleasure or pain, right or wrong, happy or unhappy. It's the space within which all of these opposites arise, and it's the final frontier in our quest for happiness.

In many religions, it's considered the sacred height of religious practice—it's the presence of Christ or direct communion with God. Spiritual philosophers have long referred to this space as "the great ground of being," the "gap," or "the field of pure consciousness." In all traditions, this state of mind is described as a place of great peace and pure, unconditional love.

I want to conclude this chapter with an exercise that could very well change your life, or at least the way you look at it, for good. It was originally developed by NLP pioneer Robert Dilts, and I've used it to make both gentle and dramatic changes in my life since I first learned it.

I recommend blocking out at least 15 minutes to do this for the first time and, if possible, doing it with a partner who can assist you. My experience of guiding several thousand people through this exercise over the past 16 years is that its effectiveness increases exponentially when you actually get up and walk through it. By engaging your body and not just your mind, the experience becomes far more profound, and the insights it produces are evoked from a much deeper place.

I've written the instructions that follow as though you're going to be exploring the context of "happiness." Once you're comfortable with the steps, you may repeat it, substituting the context of "depression," "anxiety," "guilt," "shame," or anything else you wish to explore.

Caution

Although this is a fairly robust exercise, it's not a good idea to use it to explore anything traumatic or therapeutic in nature without a qualified helping professional by your side!

---

1. Get five pieces of paper and write down each of the following terms, one to a page:

   Environment
   Behavior
   Capabilities
   Beliefs and Values
   Identity

2. Stand somewhere with at least six feet of empty space in front of you. Lay the pieces of paper out on the floor in order like a series of stepping-stones. (After you've done the exercise a few times, you'll no longer need the pieces of paper.)

3. Step into the first space marked *Environment.* Answer the following questions (and any others that seem relevant):

   - Where are you when you're happiest?

   - Where else?

   - What do you see and hear?

   - Who else (if anyone) is there with you?

4. When you have a real sense of your "happy environments," step into the second space, marked *Behavior.* Answer the following questions (and any others that seem relevant):

   - What do you do when you're feeling happy?

   - What activities do you engage in?

   - If others were watching you feeling happy on a video, what would they see you do?

   - What would they hear you say?

5. Now step into the third space, marked *Capabilities.* Answer the following questions (and any others that seem relevant):

   - What capabilities do you tap into in order to experience happiness?

   - What skills do you put into practice?

   - What areas of expertise do you draw on?

6. Next step into the space marked *Beliefs and Values.* Answer the following questions (and any others that seem relevant):

   - What's important about happiness? Why does it matter? What's most significant about it?

   - What's true about happiness? What would be the most vital thing for someone you love to know about it?

   Complete the following sentences:

   - Feeling happy is . . .

   - The most important thing about feeling happy is . . .

7. Take a step forward into the space marked *Identity.* Answer the following questions (and any others that seem relevant):

   - Who are you when you're happy?

   - Who and what else are you?

- Who are you at your best when you're feeling happy?

- Who are you at your worst when you're feeling happy?

8. Finally, take a step off the last piece of paper and into a space of unconditional love. Close your eyes and take as long as you want to connect with the best and highest thing you can imagine. You may think of that as God, your highest self, your connection with others, or simply how happiness connects with the big picture of your life. For the rest of this exercise, I'll refer to this space as "Spirit."

9. When you're ready, turn around and face back down the way you came. Carrying that sense of Spirit with you, step into the space marked *Identity*. Once again, ask and answer the question, "Who are you?" in this area of your life.

10. Bringing your sense of connectedness to Spirit and your new or heightened sense of identity with you, step into the space of *Beliefs and Values*. What seems true about happiness now? What's important about it? Why does it matter?

11. Carrying your connection to Spirit, your identity, and an awareness of your beliefs and values about happiness with you, step

back into the space of *Capabilities.* What new or additional capabilities and skills are you aware of that you draw on (or could draw on) in order to feel happy?

12. Still steeped in your connection with Spirit, identity, beliefs and values, and capabilities, step into the space of *Behavior.* What else do you do or could you do in relation to happiness? How have your answers changed? How have they stayed the same? What new things occur to you?

13. Finally, take everything you've learned and experienced about happiness back into the space of *Environment.* Where are you? Where else? What do you see? What do you hear? Who else is there with you? Who (if anyone) is no longer there?

Take all the time you need to let all the learning and changes you've experienced to integrate fully into you before you resume your normal activities. You may like to make notes about what you experienced, and you may also find that insights continue to come for hours—and sometimes days—afterward.

As we proceed into the third and final section of this book, we'll begin exploring some of the aspects of happiness that transcend simply feeling good in your body and expand into every area of your life. . . .

PART III

Feeling Happy

Chapter Eight

EMBRACING YOUR SHADOW

Coming Out of the Closet

> *"The gold is in the dark."*
> — Carl Jung

Recently I was talking with a client about her "issue": the fact that she's about to turn 40 years old in Hollywood. Her problem, or so she says, is that she looks about 30 and is terrified that if people find out her real age, she'll become unemployable. What makes her problem even more interesting (and shows how deeply paranoia can run) is that she's not even an actress; she works behind the scenes and could easily become extremely successful without anyone really knowing what she looks like.

What I suggested—somewhat tongue in cheek—was that she take out a full-page ad in *Variety* (the trade magazine for the entertainment industry) with the following copy:

[My client] would like to announce:
**I'M 40, DAMMIT, SO JUST BACK OFF AND
LEAVE ME ALONE!**

Not only would she get to stop worrying about being found out and whether or not it would really mean the end of her career, it might get her some useful publicity as well.

In every walk of life I've ever worked in or visited, people are carrying secrets—deep, dark secrets ranging from illegal activities to illicit affairs and immoral thoughts that they're convinced must never see the light of day. They'll often go to great lengths to hide these secrets, sure that the shame and suffering that would be unleashed by exposing them to the world would be devastating.

In fact, nothing could be further from the truth. In my experience, the negative energy expended in constant vigilance and the ongoing fear of being "found out" has a far more devastating effect on nearly every aspect of our lives than the secret ever could. When it comes right down to it, bringing these secrets up into the light is the most healing thing any of us can do.

Many people don't realize that the word *secret* wasn't originally a noun or an adjective but a verb. "To secret" is to separate or to keep apart. So if you're experiencing a lack of union, intimacy, love, or wholeness in your relationships or yourself, it's probably related to the act of "secreting" parts of your life away into the murky depths of your unconscious mind. And if you've been doing it long enough, you may have even been able to keep it hidden from yourself.

So how do you bring a secret up into the light?

For years, my own deepest, darkest secret was my religion. I was born a Jew into a family that (mostly) survived the ravages of living in Europe during the Second World War. Among the things I inherited was a deep paranoia about what non-Jews would do if they found out my secret. This wasn't helped by my penchant for doing the very things that Jews were technically not supposed to do. I grew up in a predominantly Catholic town, snuck off to church on Sundays, went to a Methodist university, and even did some work with an Arabian royal family, all the while hoping and praying (not Jewish prayers, mind you) that my deep, dark secret wouldn't come out.

When I dated (exclusively non-Jewish girls), there would invariably come a point where my religious heritage would come up. At that stage, I became a sort of a Jewish James Bond, thinking but rarely saying, "I could tell you, but then I'd have to kill you." Of the two women I told, I married one, thereby forcing her to take the secret with her to the grave as well!

What finally made the difference for me was recognizing that while racism (and ageism and nearly every other kind of prejudice you can imagine) clearly exists, the only reason it was a problem for me was because at some level, I agreed with it.

It wasn't other people's hate or rejection I felt and feared—it was my own. And as I learned to love and approve of myself, the hate and fear began to dissipate. Not completely, and not all at once, but enough for me to see the sun behind the clouds and recognize that the frightening shadow that I'd been hiding from was my own.

An End to Shame

If you're ready to bring your own secrets up into the light—even if it's only the light of your own conscious awareness—take some time to work through the following questions. Be gentle with yourself. If you've been "secreting" these things away for a long time, you may need to clear out a few layers of cobwebs and grit along with them.

Also, it's important to understand that you may not yet be aware of what your secrets are—if you're feeling uncomfortable about doing this exercise but aren't quite sure why, just take your time and remember that the only person who has to see any of this is you!

1. Answer as many of the following questions as honestly as you can:

    •   What are you most frightened of your partner/children/family finding out about you?

    •   What are you most frightened of your friends finding out about you?

    •   What are you most frightened of your boss or co-workers finding out about you?

    •   What are you most frightened of finding out about yourself?

    •   Which of your secrets will be discovered after you die?

    Another way of digging up your own secrets is by completing the following "sentence starters":

    •   I am embarrassed by . . .

    •   What I hate in others is . . .

    •   The worst thing anyone could say about me is . . .

This works because very often what we find most objectionable in others is a clear sign of something we're hiding away inside ourselves.

2. Identify your deepest, darkest secret—the thing that you most fear will be found out about you while you're alive or that you were planning to take with you to the grave.

3. Experiment with letting go of at least a little bit of your disapproval of yourself for whatever it is. If beating yourself up about it was going to make it better, it already would be, so see if you can offer yourself some unconditional love and approval instead. If you're finding that difficult, do the "Three Steps to Forgiveness" exercise in Chapter 9 (see page 145).

4. Choose a safe space to bring your secret out into the light for the first time. For some of you that may be with a therapist or coach; for others it might be with your family; for some it may begin with a stranger in a bar. Trust yourself—if a space feels unsafe, it's probably because it is, at least for now.

5. If some people already know your secret, who else can you share it with? The more people with whom you're able to reveal your darkness, the more light you allow into your life.

Why Not Take All of You?

> *"What we want to change in others is what*
> *we haven't loved in ourselves."*
> — Dr. John F. Demartini

A fundamental tenet of Jungian shadow work is that when you disown a part of yourself, it winds up running your life. In other words, you'll begin speaking, acting, and even pursuing certain goals in an unconscious attempt to "prove" you're not whatever your secret fear tells you that you might be.

You'll also begin to project that unowned trait onto the people around you and be amazed to suddenly find yourself living in a world populated by people who exhibit that horrible, abhorrent trait and do things that you'd "never, ever do, no matter what!"

This is one of the reasons why we have pro-lifers killing people who support abortion, relationship "experts" who can't sustain a happy marriage, and crusaders for peace waging war on the powers that be.

The flip side of this rule is what sets you free:

Once you embrace a trait, that trait
no longer runs your life.

I once heard a story about a controversial trial lawyer with a soft spot for defending underdogs and a more than 25-year record of having never lost a criminal trial.

Early in his career, the lawyer was called in to defend a black man accused of raping and murdering two white teenage girls in the Deep South. In selecting the jury, the lawyer asked each prospective juror if they were racist. With the consent of his client, he only allowed people who admitted that they were actually racist onto the jury.

His assumption was that (a) pretty much everyone who grew up in the South at that time was liable to be at least a little bit prejudiced; and (b) if individuals were willing to be honest about themselves, even if it made them look bad, they might also be willing to take an honest look at the facts instead of being blinded by their prejudice.

The same is true of each one of us—when we're willing to embrace the totality of ourselves, warts and all, we become able to live in the light of our dreams and possibilities instead of the shadow of limitations and fear.

I've played with a number of variations on the following experiment over the years. All I can tell you is that if you're willing to take it on, it's intensely liberating (and often very, very funny).

Creating "Shadow Affirmations"

1. What's your secret fear about yourself? That is, what would you least like people to find out about you?

2. What trait do you most dislike in others? What is it that other people do that makes your blood boil?

3. What's the worst thing that anyone could ever say about you?

4. Now create a "shadow affirmation" for each of the things you've come up with in the previous three questions. For example:

    - *I am a selfish bastard.*
    - *I am a self-righteous bitch.*
    - *I am a manipulative cow.*
    - *I am a complete idiot.*

    As with "real" affirmations, have some fun with this. Repeat them often, emphasizing a different word each time you say them. Make up a song and use your shadow affirmation as a lyric. (For example, try singing, *I am a selfish bastard* to the tune of "Yankee Doodle." . . .)

    Many people resist this exercise like crazy, only to find that when they give in and just do it, they wind up laughing hysterically and losing all their negative charge around the trait (or traits) they've so desperately been trying to prove aren't a part of who they are.

5. Finally, add the phrase "Sometimes . . . and sometimes I'm not" to your shadow affirmation. For example:

    • *Sometimes I am a self-righteous bitch and sometimes I'm not.*

    • *Sometimes I am a complete idiot and sometimes I'm not.*

IT'S VERY IMPORTANT NOT TO SKIP STEP FOUR. You'll lose much of the impact of the exercise should you choose to do so.

Casting a Positive Shadow

Of course, it isn't only our darkness that we tend to hide. Each of us also has a "positive shadow," filled with our disowned magnificence.

The positive shadow is made up of those positive traits you see in others but think couldn't possibly be there in you. It's the "hiding place" of your unclaimed genius, greatness, and capacity.

In the case of the positive shadow, we can see its impact in our unfulfilled aspirations, our seemingly endless quest for self-improvement, and often, surprisingly, in our personal heroes.

Whether the individuals you admire are actors or musicians ("I could never be that popular/handsome/ beautiful/wealthy/successful"); Nobel Prize winners ("I could never be that smart/powerful/influential"); or religious superstars ("I could never be that wise/spiritual/ enlightened"); we tend to put them high up on a pedestal, ensuring both that we can never reach them and that one day they'll fall from their lofty perch and we'll be crushed.

Now remember the two "rules" of embracing your shadow:

1. When you disown a part of yourself, it winds up running your life.

2. Once you embrace or "own" that part, it no longer runs your life.

To these rules, I will now add a third:

3. Whatever you admire in others, you also have within you.

The reason you haven't yet claimed the greatness within yourself may be a simple lack of recognition (that is, nobody told you to look), but it's often the lingering aftereffect of childhood hypnosis.

If the people in your life when you were growing up explicitly told you or implicitly insinuated that *you* weren't great or special or smart or creative or artistic or whatever, chances are you're still living out the belief as a sort of "posthypnotic suggestion" in your life today.

Or you may have simply hypnotized yourself into believing it, repeatedly telling yourself that you weren't capable of doing what the big people around you could do (usually because at that age, you probably weren't).

I first came across a version of the following experiment in Dr. John F. Demartini's wonderful book *The Breakthrough Experience*. It invites you to take a closer look at where you already exhibit those traits you so wish you had in your life, and it will also begin to wake you up from the "not good enough" trance that so many of us spent our childhoods living in.

Reclaiming Your Positive Shadow

1. Who are the three people you most admire in the whole world?

2. For each person, ask yourself what it is about him or her that you admire. What do people say about these folks that you wish they'd say about you?

3. What's the most flattering thing that anyone could ever say about you (even if you "know" it's not true)?

4. Instead of creating an affirmation for any positive traits you've identified, take some time to look for where you already exhibit them in your life.

   Here are some questions to get you started:

   - *Who are at least five people who already see this trait in me?*

- *Where have I exhibited this trait in the past? Where am I exhibiting it in my life now? Where will I exhibit it in the future?*

- *In which of the following areas of my life do I express this trait?*

  a. Physical   e. Finances
  b. Mental   f. Social
  c. Spiritual   g. Family
  d. Work

Feel free to push past the first three (or three dozen) times you tell yourself, *Nobody thinks this of me, and it's not true in any area of my life.* In the same way that you may not have been able to find your keys or the salt or even your car when they were right in front of you all the time, your strengths, gifts, and genius are often hidden in plain sight until someone points them out to you.

If you really struggle with completing this experiment, you might just be too scared to truly look. Consider these famous words from the book *A Return to Love,* by author and lecturer Marianne Williamson:

Our deepest fear is not that we are inadequate. Our deepest fear is that we are powerful beyond measure. It is our light, not our darkness, that most frightens us. We ask ourselves, Who am I to be brilliant, gorgeous, talented, fabulous? Actually, who are you *not* to be? You are a child of God. Your playing small doesn't serve the world. There's nothing enlightened about shrinking so that other people won't feel insecure around you. We are all meant to shine, as children do. We were born to make manifest the glory of God that is within us. It's not just in some of us; it's in everyone. And as we let our own light shine, we unconsciously give other people permission to do the same. As we are liberated from our own fear, our presence automatically liberates others.

In the next chapter, we'll explore how "letting your light shine" works in the real world. . . .

Chapter Nine

<u>NO REGRETS</u>

A Highly Personal Path

> *"Make the most of your regrets. . . .*
> *To regret deeply is to live afresh."*
> — Henry David Thoreau

I have two pictures on the wall in my office. One is a reproduction of the hand of God giving the spark of life to Adam, an enlarged close-up based on the ceiling of the Sistine Chapel; the other is a cartoon Scooby-Doo poster signed by the original voices of Fred, Daphne, and Shaggy as well as the actors who voice SpongeBob SquarePants, Johnny Bravo, and Samurai Jack. (I played the villain in *Scooby-Doo! And the Legend of the Vampire* . . . and I would have got away with it too if it hadn't been for those meddling kids!)

As it happens, one of my favorite things in the world to do is to voice cartoons. The problem is that for years, I didn't feel it was a "worthy" profession, and I constantly threatened myself, my wife, my agent, and anyone else who'd listen that at any moment I was going to go off, quit the business, and do something worthwhile with my life.

The situation came to a head a few years ago when I was on the phone with an old friend. I was telling him about a fantastic audition that I'd just been on to play a cartoon mouse in a children's television series when he asked me if I wanted to leave immediately to join him in a risky but potentially groundbreaking peace mission to the Middle East.

When I brought the dilemma to one of my mentors, he suggested that I vividly imagine pursuing both life choices to the fullest before making a decision. . . .

I began by visualizing myself staying in Hollywood and pursuing my voice-over career with renewed vigor. In my mind, it was only a matter of time before I'd be starring in an amusing Disney series about a gopher named Sven who spoke with a lisp, and children across America would be imitating my comic delivery of Sven's controversial catchphrase: "How 'bout those crazy Yankees!"

I then imagined myself going to the Middle East and becoming actively involved in the peace process. I met more people than I could ever remember by name, saw more pain and suffering each year than I would otherwise have encountered in a lifetime, and experienced a depth of love and connection that brought tears to my eyes.

And yet . . . all I could think about was that maybe after it was all over, I'd be able to go back to Hollywood and do the children's TV show! At that moment, a story I once heard years ago came to mind:

Michelangelo was on his way to visit the Pope when he came across three stonemasons at work on the foundation of the Sistine Chapel.

When he saw the first, a somewhat dour fellow, repetitively chipping away at a huge slab of rock, the artist asked him what he was doing.

"What does it look like I'm doing?" the surly laborer replied. "I'm chipping away at a huge slab of rock."

A bit farther along, he saw another workman doing a similar job, but with a bit more focus and intent.

When questioned about what he was doing, the workman scarcely looked up. "What does it look like I'm doing?" he answered. "I'm providing a home for the woman and children I love."

Before he could go any further, Michelangelo noticed that the third stonemason was working as if possessed by joy.

"What are you doing?" asked a curious Michelangelo.

The man stopped for a moment and his smile broadened. "What does it look like I'm doing?" he replied peacefully. "I'm building a cathedral to God."

Here's what I realized:

> *How meaningful your life is has nothing to do with what you choose to do and everything to do with why and how you choose to do it.*

You can exercise to punish your body or to celebrate it. You can become a millionaire to keep yourself out of the poorhouse or as part of your contribution to the well-being of the planet. And in a way that I may never be able to explain fully, the joy that I feel in my heart when I do silly voices in front of a microphone is one of the most powerful prayers for peace that I know.

Decisions, Decisions

The fear of regret often delays or even stops us from making decisions as we paralyze ourselves with stories about "what might not be" and "what might have been." But what's interesting is that feeling good or bad about what we've decided almost always *precedes* the consequences of our decision. In other words, you don't usually wait to see how something turns out before you begin either regretting it or feeling good about it.

What's actually going on here? What do these feelings about our newly minted decisions actually tell us?

Earlier this year, I was speaking with a very good friend of mine who had to choose between two job offers, both of which would make the average employee drool. He explored the choices in great detail and then—based on a combination of researched information and expert advice—made his decision.

A few days later he called me to say, somewhat sheepishly, that he was beginning to regret what he had chosen, although his job wouldn't be starting for another week.

For myself, I find that regret (and in particular, "premature regret") nearly always corresponds to not following my inner knowing. If I've really listened to and followed my inner guidance about a situation and things still don't work out, I don't mind so much. I even have it written up on the board above my computer as a personal guideline: "Follow your inner wisdom, even when you're wrong."

But if I "know" at some level that something is wrong for me and I wind up going with it anyway, I almost instantly begin to regret it. And if I don't listen to that feeling and course-correct (by changing my direction), I wind up with consequences that I'll regret even more in the future.

In that sense, fearing regret is a bit like fearing that when you look at your compass, it will tell you that you're heading south instead of true north. It doesn't really mean anything except that it's time to turn around and move forward with your life.

Treating my friend's regret as nothing more or less than a point on his inner compass, I guided him through an exercise I call "The Decision Accelerator." By the time we were done, he had reconnected to his inner knowing and "re-decided" which job to take. What made the process truly worthwhile was that he then had both the wisdom to explore the potential consequences of his new decision (particularly to his "almost employers") and the courage to have the inevitably awkward conversations to put things right. (As a point of interest, he has now been with the new company for nearly six months and is absolutely loving it!)

Here's the exercise so you can use it to help make an important decision for yourself:

The Decision Accelerator

1. Think about a decision you have (or want) to make. To make this simpler the first time you do it, choose a decision that essentially comes down to one of two choices.

2. Imagine that you've firmly and irrevocably made choice number one. Who would you tell first? What would you say to them? What would you tell them that you're particularly looking forward to? How would they react? How do you feel in yourself about the decision you've made?

3. Now imagine that you've been living with that decision for a year. Things have gone well—not perfectly, but well. What have been the good things about the decision you made? What hasn't worked out quite as you had hoped? How do you feel in yourself about the decision now?

4. Finally, imagine that it's ten years from now and you're really, really happy in yourself and with your life. What is it about your life that you enjoy so much?

   As you think back to that decision you made all those years ago, how do you think about it now? What contribution did it make to where you are in your life today? How do your feel now about the decision you made way back then?

5. When you've completed these steps in as much detail as possible, jot down any additional thoughts or insights you may be having.

6. Repeat Steps 2–5 as if you irrevocably made the *other* choice. (If you did pick a decision with more than two possible options, repeat the steps with each choice.)

7. Based on what you've learned, what's your decision? If you haven't already, make sure you explore the practical, predictable consequences of your decision, both in the very short term and in the future.

8. Take at least one concrete action in the next 24 hours to make your decision "real." If your action brings with it an increase in the feeling of "rightness," take more action; if it brings with it an increase in the feeling of regret, either repeat the exercise or explore some additional alternatives!

Inner Wisdom

When we go against our inner wanting and knowing, we may still be able to generate good feelings in the short term, but it becomes harder and harder in the long term. Even as we're trying to paper over the cracks in our integrity with "feel good" stories and "happy techniques," we'll soon discover the truth of business-guru Stephen R. Covey's golden rule:

> *You can't "technique" your way out of a problem*
> *you behaved your way into.*

While that may seem like bad news if you find yourself in this situation now, the sooner you realize you've made a wrong turn, the easier it will be to make a right one.

I was in a meeting once where I was asked to give a real-life example of the idea that at some level, everyone intuitively knows what's right for them—not in an abstract moral way, but in a deeply personal one.

For some reason, the example I chose that morning was that a remarkable number of women I've met who had been in failed marriages at some point admitted to me that they *knew* the marriage was a mistake before (or even while) walking down the aisle.

Suddenly, one of the women in the meeting burst into tears. It turned out she was engaged to be married but knew in her heart that it wasn't what she really wanted to do; however, she was horrified and terrified at the prospect of having to tell her groom-to-be (not to mention her family) that she wanted out.

One of the core ideas in my first book is this:

> *You are the expert on you. While other people may be experts*
> *on how you're supposed to behave, only you know at a*
> *fundamental level what does (or doesn't) work for you.*

During my adolescence, I used to get a gnawing feeling in the pit of my stomach that I absolutely hated. I'd do anything I could think of to get rid of it, from eating to exercising to punching myself repeatedly in the belly.

It was only when I came across the idea of "inner signals" that the gnawing feeling began to make sense. An inner signal is a unique feeling, image, or phrase that consistently and unconsciously comes up in a set context; that is, every time you find yourself in a certain situation, you experience that feeling, flash on that image, or hear that phrase in your mind.

What I finally noticed was that the feeling in the pit of my stomach only came up when I was ignoring my inner wisdom: staying at a party when I really wanted to go home, watching TV when I knew I had work to do, or saying or doing something incompatible with my values and ideals.

As soon as I realized this, the sensation that for so long had been my enemy became my friend and guide, alerting me to incongruities in my actions long before the world had a chance to teach me a lesson in its own inimitable (and often painful) way.

Similarly, by thinking back to times when I had a sense of rightness about where I was and what I was doing, I was able to identify the unique combination of feelings, words, and images that will always let me know that even if I'm not quite sure where I'm going, I'm definitely on the right track.

Do this for yourself:

1. Think of at least three times when you've intuitively known something was right for you—a real "no-brainer" yes. What did you see, hear, and feel that let you know this was the right thing for you?

EXAMPLE: **Getting Married**

I felt a complete sense of peace throughout my body and a gentle smile in my eyes and mouth when I imagined asking her. I didn't really hear anything—it was quiet inside my head, which was remarkable in and of itself. I started seeing pictures of weddings everywhere, and they always brought a smile to my face.

2. Now, think of at least three times where you've intuitively known something was wrong for you—a real "no-brainer" no. What did you see, hear, and feel that let you know this was the wrong thing for you?

EXAMPLE: **Buying a Puppy**

I really wanted to get a puppy but the moment I walked in the room, something just felt wrong. The dogs looked gorgeous, but it was almost as though I were looking at them through a glass wall. I felt a gnawing feeling in the pit of my stomach, almost like hunger, but I had just eaten lunch. The voice in my head was going nuts, saying, *Go on, just get it—what have you got to lose?*

Chances are you'll find that there's a sense of ease, freedom, and well-being that accompanies the first set of experiences and a sense of tightness, restriction, and limitation with the second. Whatever the specifics of your own experiences, the more you familiarize yourself with your inner "yes" and "no" signals now, the easier it will be to hear (and listen) to them in the future.

Here are two further distinctions that will help you clarify your own inner knowing:

1. Toward or away? When I look back over the past ten years of trusting myself as my own best expert, the biggest "mistake" I ever made occurred when I mistook the relief of moving away from something I didn't want in my life for the inner ease that generally accompanies moving toward what I really want.

I'd become involved in a business partnership that I neither enjoyed nor was profiting from and couldn't think of an elegant way out. Quite out of the blue, I received an offer to go away for six months with a show that was touring the U.K. and Malta. I jumped at the chance, thinking to myself that I'd "solved all my problems" in one fortunate swoop.

The result?

Our house was robbed the first week of the tour, I spent every night on the road desperately trying to find a television that had more than four channels, and I missed out on a great job while I was away that would have taken my career to the next level.

Now this isn't to say that nothing bad would've happened if I had moved toward what I wanted instead of running away from what I didn't want, but I know from dozens of experiences since then that when you're actively moving toward what you really, really want, setbacks and problems fade into the background in the excitement and passion of doing what you love and loving what you do.

2. Talking yourself into or out of something. Over the years, I've learned that the moment you begin talking yourself into or out of a course of action based on logic or "sensible" reasoning, it's a sure sign that deep down you already know what to do.

In *You Can Have What You Want,* I share this useful rule of thumb:

The number of reasons you have to do something is inversely proportional to how much you actually want to do it.

In other words, if you have too many reasons to do something, chances are you don't really want to do it. But if you can't think of a great reason to do something and you really want or know to do it anyway, that's almost certainly an authentic, intuitive prompting or heartfelt desire.

Of course, all of this inner knowing is all well and good, but it also raises an important question: If we're designed to follow our inner wisdom in order to live happily, how can we feel happy now if we haven't been following it?

How to Live a Good Life

"I am thankful that thus far today I have not had any unkind thoughts or said any harsh words or done anything that I regret. However, now I need to get out of bed and so things may become more difficult."
— Sylvia Boorstein

If you want to be a "good person" and live a moral and virtuous life, you're generally advised to do two things:

1. Consciously choose your moral code.
2. Do your best to live by it.

A moral code is any collection of clear statements about what constitutes "right and wrong," "good and bad," or, depending on the code, "good and evil." One of the simplest moral codes that seems to turn up in nearly every religion is the "golden rule": "Do unto others as you would have them do unto you."

Now this is, of course, great advice, but it's in doing our best to live by it that for many of us the advice breaks down. No matter how clear we are about how we "should" live, actually living that way is considerably harder.

This is why in order to "encourage" you to live by these rules, many moral codes come with built-in punishments for violating them, ranging from feelings of guilt and prayers for repentance to eternal damnation and divine retribution.

Yet how much easier might it be to live a "good life" if we changed our two-part formula to this:

1. Consciously choose your "ground of being"—
   how you want to be in the world.

2. Do your best to live *from* it.

Mahatma Gandhi famously said, "You must be the change you want to see in the world." What if living a good life is simply the natural consequence of coming from a "good" ground of being?

The way you do this is simple:

Ground of Being

1. Think about an area in your life you'd like to change. It could be a problem at work, a relationship with a loved one, or even a situation in the world.

2. Decide how you want to be in relation to that situation. Would you like to be loving? Warm? Open? Honest? Strong? Direct? Playful? Fun?

   Whatever you decide, take a few moments now to imagine feeling exactly the way you'd like it to feel and being the way you'd like it to be.

3. Go into the interaction with the conscious intention to be the way you've chosen, and act accordingly.

When we do our best to follow the prompting of our inner signals during the day, we're blessed to be able to go to bed at night with a clear head and an easy heart.

And even if you've spent so long ignoring your inner signals that you find yourself going 180 degrees in the opposite direction of your own best life, you can choose your ground of being and change your direction right at this very moment now. . . .

The "Secret" to a Better Life

*"The day the child realizes that all adults are imperfect, he
becomes an adolescent; the day he forgives them, he becomes
an adult; the day he forgives himself, he becomes wise."*
— Alden Nowlan

A few years ago, a coach I was working with gave me
the assignment of forgiving myself each night before I
went to sleep.

Resisting the urge to launch into a lecture on why I
didn't believe in forgiveness and explain how when you've
followed your inner signals and acted with integrity there
was nothing to forgive, I decided instead to do what I ask
of my own clients: to try something out before telling me
why it doesn't work or won't work for them.

To my amazement, the very first night I came up with
nearly a dozen things that I was rerunning in my mind,
beating myself up about, and just generally hating myself
for. This put me in the uncomfortable position of realizing
that I'd spent so long disavowing the practice of forgiveness,
I'd never taken the time to learn how to do it.

A quick trip to the dictionary brought me this definiton:

for•give
(fər-'giv, fór-)
1. To excuse for a fault or an offense
2. To renounce anger or resentment against
3. To absolve from payment of a debt, financial or
   otherwise

As I explored each of these meanings, I recognized that
the common theme was "to let go." This raised two more

questions: First, *why* should I let go of (excuse/renounce/ absolve) my anger, resentment, and the debts I feel that I'm owed; and second, if and when I do decide to let go, *how* do I actually do it?

1. To Let Go or Not to Let Go

Forgiveness is one of those annoying things that "good people" are meant to do, which both turns it into an obligation (and don't you just hate obligations?) and disguises the fact that forgiveness isn't a remotely selfless act.

Holding on to anger and resentment is exhausting and can make us physically ill over time, while doing nothing to the well-being of the people we believe we are punishing in some way by holding on to the anger and resentment.

Doc Childre, researcher and founder of the Institute of HeartMath, puts it quite beautifully in his book *The HeartMath Solution:*

> In the long run, it's not a question of whether someone *deserves* to be forgiven. You're not forgiving your transgressor for his or her sake; you're doing it for yourself. Forgiveness is simply the most energy-efficient option you face, and the only one that will foster health and well-being. It frees you from the toxic, debilitating drain of holding a grudge. Don't let villains live rent-free in your head. If they've hurt you in the past, why let them keep hurting you year after year in your mind?

2. How to Forgive

Several years ago, I began studying with a man named Larry Crane, co-creator with Lester Levenson of "The Abundance Course." In his public talks, Larry teaches a simple three-step process that he recommends for everything from healing pain to enhancing relationships to increasing happiness, prosperity, and abundance.

When I began to explore the question of "how to forgive," I suddenly recognized that the steps to forgiveness were the same as the ones in Larry's "Cure All" process—and they work almost as quickly as you're willing to try them out for yourself. . . .

a. Let go of trying to figure things out. One of the ways we keep painful reactions alive in our systems is by endlessly trying to figure out "why" things turned out the way they did and what we could have been done differently. Now if you do this in a focused way—in order to learn from what happened—this can be a very useful process. Unfortunately, most people do it in a semiconscious, endless loop of half thoughts and ever-changing conclusions.

When you let go of trying to figure things out, you're left with what is—and although you might not like it, you can finally face it full on.

b. Let go of disapproving of yourself (or the other person or situation). There are only two reasons why people disapprove of themselves. The first is to prove to themselves and/or others that they're "good" people, even if they've done something that might be perceived as bad. After all, if they didn't feel bad about it, people might believe that they think it's okay to think, say, or do what they've thought, said, or done.

The second reason is in order to motivate themselves to behave differently in the future. This is the legacy of generations of well-meaning parents and teachers motivating their children and charges with threats of punishment and promises of reward. But in the end, not only does this type of punishment and reward-based motivation lead to totally self-involved adults (that is, the only consequence that matters to them is the consequence to themselves), it rarely works.

Let's look at a quick example. . . .

Perhaps when you're feeling anxious, you eat rapidly until you can feel your system start to slow down and relax. But a few minutes later, that relaxed feeling has turned into exhaustion, and you can feel yourself slipping into a food coma. When you eventually come out of your self-induced catatonic state, your inner storyteller begins to beat you up so that you'll never be so "bad" again. Your blood pressure increases and your anxiety levels begin to rise. . . .

What happens next?

Do you keep your resolution to "never overeat again"? Or do you throw yourself naked into the refrigerator, eating your way through the top three shelves in order to once again restore your system to some semblance of calm well-being until after the next food coma when the whole sequence begins again?

When you decide that disapproving of yourself will neither make you a better person nor enhance your ability to go for what you want, the disapproval will begin to disappear all by itself.

c. Give yourself approval. Even after exploring the previous two steps for themselves, many people still think it's absurd to go so far as to give themselves or others approval for what they believe are their failings, faults, and foul-ups. But perhaps the greatest secret in life is this:

There is nothing wrong with you.

Except for the stories you may be telling yourself about how you're supposed to be, what you're supposed to be doing, and who you're supposed to (or not supposed to) be doing it with, *you are perfect exactly as you are.*

To give yourself approval for being as you are is to accept that you're a spiritual being having a human experience— and like a $100 bill that's been through the mud and the wash and a dozen people's pockets, your value doesn't diminish regardless of what you've been through in your life.

Try this exercise for yourself and notice what you notice:

Three Steps to Forgiveness

1. Make a list of resentments or grudges that you're carrying around against other people or life in general. Notice whether you'd be willing to let go of (forgive) each of these in turn.

   For any where the answer is "no," ask yourself if you're hanging on (a) because it would mean something bad about you if you didn't; (b) to make sure that "it" doesn't happen again; or (c) both of the above.

Remember, you're under no obligation to forgive—it's simply a choice that only you can make and only for your own well-being.

2. Before you go to sleep this evening, make a mental or physical list of anything that you're mad at yourself for and/or beating yourself up about.

Take each one through the three steps of forgiveness:

a. Let go of trying to figure it out.

b. Let go of disapproving of yourself for it.

c. Give yourself approval—no conditions, no judgments, and no expectations.

When you first start to forgive yourself and everyone around you, it may seem as if the list of people and things to forgive will go on forever. But before long, you'll feel a level of clarity and peace about your life that makes you realize that in many cases, there's nothing to forgive.

It's at this point that you begin to access a new power within yourself—a power that heals even the deepest wounds and gives you the opportunity to become whole again. . . .

Chapter Ten

THE HEALING POWER OF COMPASSION

What's So Funny 'bout Peace, Love, and Understanding?

"It is not the threat of death, illness, hardship, or poverty that crushes the human spirit; it is the fear of being alone and unloved in the universe."
— Anthony Welsh

Over breakfast one morning, I attempted to answer my daughter's questions about what to do if she didn't enjoy the Nativity play we were going to see.

After listening to my answer, which was a somewhat garbled attempt at explaining the importance of balancing a commitment to honesty in ourselves with compassion for the best efforts of others (admittedly a bit "out there" for a four-year-old), my wife began to tease me.

"And if we all just loved each other a little bit more," she said, tongue firmly in cheek, "wouldn't the world be a better place?"

Well, as it happens, I believe it would be. Why I believe this, and why I've committed my life to sharing this point of view may take a bit of explaining. . . .

On a school trip to Israel at the age of 13, my classmates and I were taken to a place I've been told no longer exists in the midst of central Jerusalem called the Museum of the Future Holocaust. At the end of our tour detailing the horrors of racism and anti-Semitism throughout the world, we were shown a film that focused on the continued presence and ongoing atrocities of hate groups within the United States—particularly focusing on the actions of the Ku Klux Klan and the American Nazi Party.

By the time the museum "guide" stopped the film to solicit our reactions, I was so angry, outraged, frightened, and confused that I could barely speak. In time, I managed to choke out that if someone had walked into the room right then wearing a Nazi uniform or a white hood, I'd have killed them on the spot using any means at my disposal.

What I remember most vividly was everyone's calm reaction to my confession, as if that were the only sane response to what we'd just seen. I had expected them to share in the horror of my startling realization: I would have made a great Nazi. After all, if I could be persuaded to hate nameless, faceless groups of individuals on the basis of a one-hour propaganda film, then what could I have been persuaded to do if I'd been exposed to teachings of hate and intolerance from the moment I was born?

I was suddenly faced with a choice: to deny my uncomfortable realization that I, too, could fill up with hate and be taught to kill, or to reject my comfortable ideas of good and evil and begin to see the "enemy" as unhappy, frightened human beings just like me whose ideas about good and evil had been shaped by the people around them—just like mine.

But how do you feel love and compassion for people you were brought up to hate? Harder still, what if they also really hate you?

Whenever I bring up the possibility of choosing love

and compassion, someone invariably asks some variation of: "What about bin Laden? You want me to love *him?*"

Asking ourselves to love bin Laden, Hitler, or any other world leader who espouses hatred, particularly hatred of the things we hold dear, is equivalent to asking a novice pianist to play a Rachmaninoff concerto. Blindfolded. With one hand.

You learn to play the piano by practicing scales. And you learn to choose love by practicing compassionate understanding, recognizing the us in "them" and the "them" in us.

The first time I really understood this was when I heard the story of Marge Knuuti, a nurse and teacher who decided to do volunteer work at Mother Teresa's Home for the Dying in Calcutta.

After many hours spent on old train tracks and bumpy roads in the heat of the Indian summer, she arrived exhausted, wanting nothing more than to jump into a cold shower and collapse into a cool bed.

Instead, she was greeted by the scene of dozens of people lined up outside in the hope of being given the right to die with dignity and compassion. Her tiredness fell away, and she reached out to a man whose legs had been crushed in the street and whose life was clearly ebbing away. As she looked into his eyes brimming with love and compassion, he kept repeating the word *namaste* to her.

Many hours later, she asked one of the other volunteers what it meant. She was told that it was a Sanskrit word signifying:

> *I honor the place in you where the entire Universe resides. I honor the place in you of love, of truth, of peace, and of light; and when you are in that place in you and I am in that place in me, there is only one of us.*

A Compassionate Practice

*"Our strength will continue if we allow ourselves the courage
to feel scared, weak, and vulnerable."*
— Melody Beattie

One of the few perks of going through a period of loss, crisis, and/or suffering is that when you come out the other side (and nearly everyone does, sooner or later), you realize that you're a lot stronger than you probably thought you were. Better still, that strength doesn't leave you even after the crisis has passed.

My first real experience of this came during the second year of my theater degree studies when a group of my fellow students and I were placed on probation for the final six weeks of the school year.

Whoever got it together and performed well in the final productions would remain in the professional actor training program and ultimately audition for the top agents and casting directors in New York and Los Angeles; the rest would be downgraded to a "Theater Arts" curriculum where they'd spend their time studying the role of politics in the works of Bertolt Brecht instead of actually getting to ply their craft.

So stressful was this "sorting" process on our postadolescent minds that in my year alone, there were two attempted suicides and one guy (who happened to be my best friend) committed to a mental institution.

Although I'd like to say I handled the situation with ease and grace, the reality is that I spent the early part of the six weeks drunk. I followed my lunchtime margarita with nightly happy-hour 2-for-1 specials, which carried me through evening rehearsals and—on one or two unfortunate occasions—the performances themselves.

Samuel Johnson once said, "When a man knows he is to be hanged in a fortnight, it concentrates his mind wonderfully"; and as the day of decision grew closer and closer, it became apparent to me that I wasn't the only one suffering. To my surprise, I realized that if I were to make it through and my fellow actors didn't, I'd feel their pain as acutely as I did my own.

It was around this time that I was introduced to the ancient Buddhist practice of Tonglen, a meditation that brings compassion to life by asking the practitioner to breathe in the pain and suffering of others and breathe out kindness, love, and compassion.

Unlike the advice of most of the well-meaning people around me and my own instinct to avoid my pain at any cost, Tonglen invited me to not only feel the pain completely, but to seek out more of it in the people around me.

With each inhale, I'd breathe in their suffering and sorrow, anger and loss, sadness and despair; with each exhale, I'd direct as much love, happiness, and good feeling as I could find inside me back out into the world.

While part of me thought it was nuts to deal with my own pain by taking on even more of it, the reality was that the more I practiced, the better I felt. If I was going to go down—and I was sure I was at the time—I was not only not going to drag anyone else along with me, I was going to do all that I could to ensure that I went down alone.

Recently I came across a photo I took of the panel of teachers whom I had to face on the final day of the term, posed in mock seriousness like a firing squad. When they told me that I'd been chosen to remain in the program, I was ecstatic, but I burst into tears of disbelief when they said what had convinced them was my incredible strength throughout the ordeal.

I didn't feel strong. I didn't feel worthy. I didn't "think positive" or "believe in myself." But I did survive, and I did make it through—and better still, a few of my compatriots whose own fear, worry, and sadness I had breathed in on a daily basis made it through along with me.

What I learned was not only that I was a lot stronger than I originally thought, but that I could find that strength most easily when I used it to support the people around me. And while I wouldn't wish what I went through on my worst enemy, I'm eternally glad that I went through it.

In the following experiment, I'll introduce you to the steps of Tonglen so you can begin to experience it for yourself. As with many practices, it's far easier to do than to understand, so be patient and allow yourself a bit of time with this one. . . .

Tonglen

1. Open yourself up to the wholeness of the universe—the space in which birth and death, joy and suffering, and war and peace continually arise and fall away.

2. From this place, breathe in the "texture" of suffering. You may imagine this as thick, heavy, dark smoke. Each time you exhale, breathe out the texture of love, kindness, and compassion. Many people experience this as clear and bright, light and refreshing.

3. When you have a sense for yourself of the transformation of energy happening inside you, think of a specific individual or an incident to work with. This can be a stranger you saw in the street, someone you know intimately, or even yourself.

   Now, with each inhale, breathe in the pain of that person or incident; with each exhale, direct the energy of love, compassion, and kindness back to that person or incident.

4. Finish your practice by extending transformational compassion to the wider world: Breathe in the suffering of the planet, and breathe out well-being, love, and peace.

There is an ancient Cherokee story about a tribal elder who is teaching his grandson about life:

"A fight is going on inside me," he said to the boy. "It is a terrible fight between two wolves.

"One is evil—he is anger, envy, sorrow, regret, greed, arrogance, self-pity, guilt, resentment, inferiority, deception, false pride, superiority, and ego.

"The other is good—he is joy, peace, love, hope, serenity, humility, kindness, benevolence, empathy, generosity, truth, compassion, and faith.

"This same fight is going on inside you, and inside every other person, too."

The boy thought about it for a minute, and then asked his grandfather, "Which wolf will win?"

The old Cherokee simply replied, "The one you feed."

Chapter Eleven

THE GIFT OF GRATITUDE

On Thanksgiving

> *"Be kind. Everyone you meet is fighting a hard fight."*
> — John Watson

I recently came across some unpublished writings by Benjamin Franklin on the origins of Thanksgiving Day. Apparently the tradition of the early Pilgrims was to spend days fasting and praying in order to plead with God for relief from their many difficulties and hardships.

One day, when yet another round of fasting and pleading was about to begin, a "Farmer of plain Sense" proposed that as "their Seas and Rivers were full of Fish, the Air sweet, the Climate healthy, and above all, they were in the full Enjoyment of Liberty, civil and religious," perhaps "it would be more becoming the Gratitude they owed to the divine Being, if instead of a Fast they should proclaim a Thanksgiving."

The farmer's advice was taken, and a day of thanks was declared.

Yet despite (or perhaps because of) growing up in a country that mandated thanksgiving, I've never been terribly good at giving thanks. One of the more infamous stories from my childhood involved my saying, "Thank you for the yucky present" to my favorite aunt and uncle, which—while it does get me points for honesty—seems a bit churlish in retrospect.

Here are some of the reasons I've been taught why I'm supposed to be grateful:

1. Being grateful will make me beloved of God. My wife, who is brilliant at thanksgiving (both the holiday and the act) equates gratitude with worship. In this sense, giving thanks for the good things we have is an acknowledgment of God's presence and impact on our lives.

2. Being grateful will make me happy. If you were to ask the three happiest people you know why it is they're so darn happy, you'd no doubt find a sense of gratitude and appreciation for what they have in their lives high on their list of causal principles. In fact, extensive research in the field of positive psychology has scientifically confirmed that not only does gratitude feel good, it also contributes to an ongoing sense of happiness and well-being in life.

3. Being grateful will make me rich. Some people aren't comfortable with stating it this bluntly, but there's a general acknowledgment in metaphysical circles that "an attitude of gratitude" is one of the fundamental keys to wealth. The more you appreciate what you have, the more it will appreciate; and that is as true with money as it is with love, talent, and friendship.

So if I have everything to gain and seemingly nothing to lose by being grateful, what is it that makes saying "Thank you"—and, indeed, the whole notion of gratitude—so difficult for me?

If I put my judgmental "I suck as a human being" hat on, it's stubborn pride and ego. The reason I'm not more naturally and expressively appreciative is quite simply because people have always told me that I'm supposed to be, and like a lot of overgrown five-year-olds, I chafe at doing what I'm told.

But if I put my compassionate "I'm good enough, I'm smart enough, and doggone it, people like me" hat on, something different emerges:

> *The reason why I'm not more openly grateful is that I'm terrified of acknowledging how much of what I have in life is mine either by chance or the grace of God—not as the result of my hard work or "positive mental attitude."*

The Myth of Self-Sufficiency

> *"There is no such thing as a 'self-made' man. We are made up of thousands of others. Everyone who has ever done a kind deed for us, or spoken one word of encouragement to us, has entered into the make-up of our character and of our thoughts, as well as our success."*
> — George Matthew Adams

Particularly in America, "independence" has long been touted as the most prized stage of development. We go out and earn our own money, make our own way, and "don't have to depend on no one for nothing"!

But while feeling able to take care of oneself is a wonderful milestone in any individual's development, at some point most of us come to realize that there's no such thing as true "independence."

Unless you harvest your own grain and nuts and grind them with stones ripped from the ground with your own bare hands, every time you have a peanut-butter sandwich, you're benefiting from the work of dozens of others who've made the raw ingredients available to you. (Not to mention the employers and/or customers who've exchanged their money with you so that you could buy those raw ingredients from the shop.)

Anyone who's ever lost a job, a fortune, or a loved one knows that when the chips are down, the first thing you realize is that not only do you not have control over what happens to you, they're not even your chips. And what could be more terrifying than acknowledging that everything you've achieved and everything you have could be taken away from you in a heartbeat?

The reality is that it isn't all up to you—but it's not all up to someone or something else either. When we combine personal responsibility with an awareness of our interdependence, we put the "I" back in "team" and free ourselves up to live happily in the world.

This reminds me of one of my favorite stories:

A minister was driving through the country when he came across a truly glorious farm being tended to by a lone farmer.

Keen to remind the farmer of the source of his blessings, the minister pulled over to the side of the road and called the farmer over.

"The Lord has blessed you with a beautiful farm," said the minister.

After a few moments' reflection, the farmer nodded his assent.

"He certainly has, Reverend—but you should have seen it when He had it all to Himself!"

Why Me?

Many years ago, I was hiking in the Berkshire mountains of Western Massachusetts with four men, all of whom had autistic children. I expected the conversation to be a commiseration of woe, and even mentally prepared some of my own sad stories to share so that I might "fit in." To my amazement, they each in turn expressed their heartfelt opinion that having an autistic child was the greatest thing that had ever happened to them.

One man spoke of how dealing with his daughter's illness had led him to reevaluate his priorities and leave a job he hated in order to spend more time with his family. Another told me that he and his wife's commitment to accepting and dealing with their son's autism had saved their marriage. The third man shared how his previously rebellious teenage children from an earlier relationship had come back into his life as they shared in the care and responsibility for their autistic sister; and the last man said that when his son finally made eye contact with him after more than a year of working with him, he rediscovered his faith.

When I finally processed that their common joy wasn't the product of "happy-clappy positive thinking," but a genuine expression of gratitude for what seemed to me to be the tragedy of their lives, I remembered a conversation with a client who had lost her baby less than a year after he was born. She had told me that what she came to realize as she passed through her own unique version of the five stages of grief was that having a child had given her access to a kind of love she'd never imagined possible. Even though her baby was no longer with her, she could still feel that extraordinary love whenever she thought of him—that had been her baby's gift to her.

I thought of that woman many years later in the midst of a more mundane challenge to my happiness and well-being. After eight hours of packing, driving, flying, and waiting in various airport lines, my family and I arrived back in Los Angeles physically intact but emotionally a bit worse for wear.

It was at this point—standing in yet another line with a screaming toddler in my arms—that my then six-year-old daughter, Clara, decided she absolutely had to have a look at her passport picture. This was a seemingly innocuous request but, in fact, would've involved my unhooking several bags from my shoulders and letting loose the toddler who, screaming aside, had already demonstrated her intention to leave no Do Not Enter sign undisturbed in her exploration of the world of airport immigration.

Now it would've been the easiest thing in the world to have thought *Why me?* when Clara was nipping at my ankles and the people in the line were silently nominating me for the "Person I'd Most Like to Not Sit Next To on an Airplane" award.

But after responding to Clara's continual requests like a six-year-old adult (I believe the words, "I'm not going to do it and you can't make me!" may have passed my lips), I took a deep breath, recognized that my reaction was more a function of my emotional state than her behavior, and apologized for being mean to her.

"Mean?" she asked incredulously. "You weren't mean to me. You're my daddy. Daddies can't be mean."

It was at this point that the question *Why me?* popped into my head. Why me? Why do I get to be loved so unconditionally by someone who's all too frequently in the line of fire when I lose my cool? How is it possible that her love and trust are still firmly intact after years of sporadically positive parenting?

There's a notion in Jewish mysticism that the nature of the universe isn't one of reward and punishment but rather one of receiving or rejecting God's blessings. When we connect with our sense of value in the world and connection to others and to life, we become like God—we share naturally and receive continually. When we cut off from our awareness of being of value and a part of all things, we become distinctly human. We retreat into ourselves and experience a world of pain, loss, and suffering.

Maybe when good things happen to me, it's not so much a reward for good behavior as a case of an abundant universe sharing freely with one of its citizens. Maybe the reason I have a daughter who loves me unconditionally is to make it easier for me to be a really great father to her. And if you find yourself to be happy or beautiful or successful or talented or wealthy, maybe it's so that you'll be able to share your happiness, beauty, talent, and wealth with the world.

When my own father was struck by a car and killed many years ago, I felt more anger, sadness, and guilt than I knew I had inside me. Because I didn't yet have an effective way of processing that pain, I dealt with it by cutting myself off from my emotions. When my own son was born a few years later, my heart cracked back open. I was so overwhelmed with love that I forgot that I "needed" to protect myself from my own feelings. To my surprise, rather than being crushed by the sorrow I'd been holding back for all those years, I began to feel whole again.

I find it an incredibly comforting thought that it's possible to come out on the other side of any tragedy enriched with more love, gratitude, and faith than we had going in.

And that, at long last, is something I can choose to be grateful for all by myself.

If you're ready to look for some "blessings in disguise" in your own life, I've found the following exercise to be an extremely valuable one.

Experimental Gratitude

1. Choose an experience that you currently view as a tragedy but are willing to see differently.

2. List at least 20 things about that experience that you see as bad or terrible.

3. Now jot down at least 20 blessings that have come from the experience. These may include positive changes in you, other people, or the world.

4. Look at both lists. Recognize that they're both likely to be "true"—accurate yet incomplete ways of perceiving the experience. Choose which list to focus on now.

5. Write a thank-you letter to the other person, God, or the universe for the blessings.

In our final chapter together, we'll take a look at the incredible difference that being happy in ourselves can ultimately make in the world around us. . . .

Chapter Twelve

THE ULTIMATE EXPERIMENT

The Story of Guinea Pig B

"People say that what we're all seeking is a meaning for life. I don't think that's what we're really seeking. I think that what we're seeking is an experience of being alive."
— Joseph Campbell

In the autumn of 1927, a man was standing at the banks of Lake Michigan. His firstborn daughter had died in his arms, his business was collapsing, and he couldn't see how he'd be able to care for his wife and newborn baby. His plan was to rid his family of "the burden of his presence" by swimming out toward the center of the freezing lake until he died of exhaustion and hypothermia.

But something unexpected happened instead. He was surrounded by light and heard a voice inside so clearly he remembered the words it spoke verbatim:

"You do not have the right to eliminate yourself," said the voice. "You belong to the universe. Your significance will remain forever obscure to you, but you may assume that you are fulfilling your role if you apply yourself to converting your experiences to the highest advantage of others."

From that moment forward, he decided to live his life as an experiment "to determine and document what one individual could accomplish on behalf of all humanity that could not be accomplished by any organization, government or business, regardless of its size and power."

He resolved to never again work for his own advantage, but only for all others for whom his "experience gained" knowledge might be of benefit, and to take great care with what he said and to whom he spoke. Taking his resolutions to heart, he lived a vow of silence for the next two years, determined not to break it until he had something truly worthwhile to say that sprang solely from his own experience—and not from what he'd been "taught" by a well-meaning but misguided world.

He even took on a new name for himself befitting his role in this ultimate experiment: Guinea Pig B.

What began in a moment of self-described "egocide" on the banks of an icy lake in Chicago became a 56-year experiment that touched the lives of millions and spawned such "artifacts" as:

- 28 U.S. patents

- More than 30 books

- 47 honorary doctorates in the arts, science, engineering, and the humanities

- Dozens of major architectural and design awards including, among many others, the Gold Medal of the American Institute of Architects and the Royal Gold Medal of the Royal Institute of British Architects

- Works that made it into the permanent collections of museums around the world

- A life that circled the globe 57 times

Guinea Pig B, known to the world as R. Buckminster Fuller, revolutionized the fields of architecture, philosophy, and art.

He invented the geodesic dome, the world's strongest man-made structure; and through his philosophical work on "how and why humans are here as passengers aboard this spherical spaceship we call Earth," he inspired the lives and innovations of a generation of artists, world leaders, and thinkers.

Perhaps even more impressive than his accomplishments is the extraordinary impact he had on nearly everyone who met him. As happiness guru Barry Neil Kaufman has written:

> Imagine the impact on a nation
> by a happy and loving head of state,
> on an army by a happy and loving general,
> on children by a happy and loving parent,
> on a relationship by a happy and loving spouse,
> on a patient by a happy and loving nurse,
> or on a student by a happy and loving teacher.

I think of this every time I question the value of happiness as a worthy goal. Inevitably, I realize that it isn't just what we do when we're happy, but our happiness itself that makes a difference in the world.

The more grounded you are in your well-being and the more willing you are to live life on your own terms, the greater the impact you'll have on each and every one of the people around you.

What One Person Can Do

> *"God heard us. He sent help. He sent you."*
> — Marianne Williamson

Many years ago (or so the story goes) in a time of great war and consternation, there was a monastery that had fallen upon hard times. There were few monks left, and they tended to squabble among themselves. Everyone was convinced that their path was the right one, and the peaceful ways of the past seemed little more than a dream.

In a last-ditch attempt to save the monastery, the abbot sought the advice of an old rabbi, who was reputed to have immense wisdom and insight into the workings of humanity.

When the abbot told the rabbi of the situation, he shook his head with great concern. "It's imperative that you find a way to resolve this situation before it's too late," said the rabbi. "For what you don't realize is that among you is the One who will deliver us all from fear into love."

The abbot asked who among them was the One, but the rabbi would tell him no more. On the way back to the monastery, he wondered who the One could be. "I bet it's Brother Arthur," he thought to himself. "He is kind and good. Or perhaps it's Brother Thomas— he's young but already shows great wisdom. Or could it be . . . no . . . I mustn't even consider that it might be me!"

On his return, the abbot shared the news with the monks. Although they were startled, there was a ring of truth to what he had said. The One was among them!

As they contemplated which of them it might be, the monks began to treat one another with a very special reverence and respect. After all, someone among them might really be the One. And, on the off chance that each monk himself might be the One, they began to treat themselves with extraordinary respect and reverence as well.

As time went by, the monks developed a gentle, loving quality, which was hard to quantify but easy to notice. They lived respectfully, in harmony with themselves and nature. An aura of peace and reverence seemed to radiate out from them and permeate the atmosphere. There was something strangely attractive, even compelling about it.

Before long, people were coming from far and wide to be nourished by the life of the monks, and young men were asking to become a part of their community.

Within a few short years, the monastery had once again become home to a thriving order—a vibrant center of light and spirituality in the world.

If you knew that you really mattered—that your life was essential to the well-being of the planet—what would you do to cultivate your own happiness and well-being? What would you stop doing? What would you do more of? What would you do less of?

If you knew that each person you met today could be the One, how would you treat them?

Be aware that anyone and anything you treat with reverence becomes sacred—and that includes both you and your life.

I began this book with a quote from the playwright and social activist George Bernard Shaw. Here it is in its entirety:

> This is the true joy in life, the being used for a purpose recognized by yourself as a mighty one; the being thoroughly worn out before you are thrown on the scrap heap; the being a force of Nature instead of a feverish selfish little clod of ailments and grievances complaining that the world will not devote itself to making you happy. . . .
>
> I am of the opinion that my life belongs to the whole community and as long as I can live it is my privilege to do for it what I can. I want to be thoroughly used up when I die, for the harder I work, the more I live. I rejoice in life for its own sake.

Life is no "brief candle" to me. It is a sort of splendid torch which I have got hold of for the moment, and I want to make it burn as brightly as possible before handing it on to future generations.

As you contemplate what kind of vision, purpose, or mission would get you jumping out of bed in the morning and forcing yourself to get back in it at night, here's an experiment in finding the true joy in life that can go on for at least as long as you do. . . .

A Life-Changing Experiment

1. Imagine that your life up until now has been an experiment. What has it been an experiment in?
    Examples:

    -   How far can one person go without paying attention to their life?

    -   How long can one person maintain an intimate relationship without demonstrating respect for their partner?

    -   How much blame, shame, and guilt can one person experience before they completely self-destruct?

2. Choose an experiment that's worth committing your life to—your very own "ultimate experiment"!

Examples:

- How far can I advance in my career while staying 100 percent true to my values?

- If I found more peace within myself, would it lead to more peace in the world?

- What's the difference that I can make in the lives of others by simply loving them unconditionally and believing in their ability to make choices and lead radically different lives?

Some Final Thoughts on Feeling Happy Now

When I first share the ideas we've been exploring together in this book, there's often a palpable excitement as people begin to experience their own power to create and live from a place of happiness and well-being inside themselves.

Occasionally, someone will ask whether using these tools will mean that they'll never feel unhappy again. Fortunately, the answer is no—I've yet to come across a lasting, meaningful happiness that doesn't include the full spectrum of experience and emotion. But I know for myself the joy of a life that gets better and better as I become happier and happier.

Think about it like this. You've probably seen this classic drawing of the cycles of most of the body's natural rhythms:

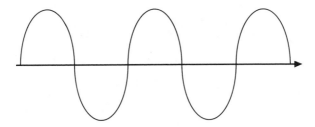

Now notice what happens if you accept the ups and downs of your daily rhythms, but you experience them in the context of an ongoing program for increasing your happiness and well-being:

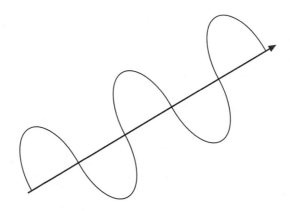

Your highs become higher, and your lows become higher as well. Over time, what was once a 10 on your scale of happiness can become your new 1. It is, perhaps, an unreasonable goal—but in my experience, all the best goals inevitably are.

Here's one last thought experiment to take with you as you continue on your journey. . . .

Take a few moments now to love and appreciate whatever it is that you love and appreciate about yourself. You can expand that love to include your immediate family members and close friends. Continue expanding in love to include what you love and appreciate about your home, neighborhood, community, country, planet, universe, and whatever concept of the words *God* or *Spirit* or *Unconditional Love* that you find most meaningful to you.

Now . . . open up to receive all that love back, knowing that the mathematics of love are exponential—whatever you give away comes back multiplied. Imagine the love that God/Spirit/ Unconditional Love has for you. Imagine being loved by the universe, loved by the Earth, and loved by your country.

Open up to the idea of being loved and appreciated by your community, loved and appreciated by your neighborhood, and loved and appreciated in your home. And as you imagine being loved and appreciated by the people you care about most, finish once again by feeling— really feeling—the love and appreciation you have for whatever it is you love and appreciate about yourself.

I'll close with the words of the person who's taught me more about love and happiness than anyone else—my wife, Nina:

"(S)he who dies with the most love wins!"

Until we meet,

Michael

Appendix

TO BE OPENED IN CASE OF EMERGENCY

"There is chaos under the heavens
and the situation is excellent."
— Chinese proverb

While it would be nice to believe that reading this book would be enough to inoculate you against the slings and arrows of outrageous fortune, I live in the real world—a world where nothing lasts, no one gets out alive, and bad things happen to good people. (In fairness, they also happen to "bad" people in roughly the same proportion, a fact that seems to elude most observers.)

This impartial "karma" isn't noticed because from an early age, we're taught to take things personally—that not only do we have the power to make the people around us happy, but they have the power to make us very unhappy indeed.

But what happens when you stop taking things personally—when you let go of the story that God, the universe, or the wheel of karma has singled you out to be flung up to the heights or down to the depths as punishment or reward for what you did or didn't do in this life or the last?

I remember finding great inspiration in the words of Holocaust survivor Viktor Frankl, describing a long march in the dead of winter through the death camps of Auschwitz:

> A thought transfixed me: for the first time in my life I saw the truth as it is set into song by so many poets, proclaimed as the final wisdom by so many thinkers. The truth—that love is the ultimate and the highest goal to which man can aspire. Then I grasped the meaning of the greatest secret that human poetry and human thought and belief have to impart: *The salvation of man is through love and in love.* I understood how a man who has nothing left in this world may still know bliss, be it only for a brief moment, in the contemplation of his beloved. In a position of utter desolation, when a man cannot express himself in positive action, when his only achievement may consist in enduring his sufferings in the right way—an honorable way—in such a position man can, through loving contemplation of the image he carries of his beloved, achieve fulfilment. For the first time in my life I was able to understand the words, "The angels are lost in perpetual contemplation of an infinite glory."

When I first read that passage, I figured that if people could find moments of happiness in a concentration camp, then I could probably find a few in the midst of paradise.

❖ ❖ ❖

Here's a reminder of the key formulas, recipes, experiments, and techniques that will help you feel happy and cared for even in the midst of the emergencies and crises of your life:

> The Happy Formula (page 7)
> The Permission Principle (page 25)
> A Recipe for Feeling Good (page 29)
> The NOW Exercise (page 50)
> The Practice of Nonmeditation (page 54)
> Be Your Own "Spin Doctor" (page 76)
> Mickey Mouse Therapy (page 79)
> Three Steps to Forgiveness (page 145)
> Tonglen (page 152)

Finally, here is a treasure I personally use whenever I need to balance my perceptions and renew my spirit: the "Desiderata" by the German-American poet Max Ehrmann:

> *Go placidly amid the noise and haste,*
> *and remember what peace there may be in silence.*
> *As far as possible without surrender*
> *be on good terms with all persons.*
> *Speak your truth quietly and clearly;*
> *and listen to others,*
> *even the dull and the ignorant;*
> *they too have their story.*
>
> *Avoid loud and aggressive persons,*
> *they are vexations to the spirit.*
> *If you compare yourself with others,*
> *you may become vain and bitter;*

*for always there will be greater and lesser persons than
yourself.
Enjoy your achievements as well as your plans.*

*Keep interested in your own career, however humble;
it is a real possession in the changing fortunes of time.
Exercise caution in your business affairs;
for the world is full of trickery.
But let this not blind you to what virtue there is;
many persons strive for high ideals;
and everywhere life is full of heroism.*

*Be yourself.
Especially, do not feign affection.
Neither be cynical about love;
for in the face of all aridity and disenchantment
it is as perennial as the grass.*

*Take kindly the counsel of the years,
gracefully surrendering the things of youth.
Nurture strength of spirit to shield you in sudden
misfortune.
But do not distress yourself with dark imaginings.
Many fears are born of fatigue and loneliness.
Beyond a wholesome discipline,
be gentle with yourself.*

*You are a child of the universe,
no less than the trees and the stars;
you have a right to be here.
And whether or not it is clear to you,
no doubt the universe is unfolding as it should.*

Therefore be at peace with God,
whatever you conceive Him to be,
and whatever your labors and aspirations,
in the noisy confusion of life keep peace with your soul.

With all its sham, drudgery, and broken dreams,
it is still a beautiful world.
Be cheerful.
Strive to be happy.

WANT TO LEARN MORE?

I've collected some of my favorite resources for creating happiness at my Website. Please visit: **www.geniuscatalyst.com/happy.php**.

If you'd like to join the Genius Catalyst community and have access to hundreds of tips, podcasts, e-programs, and additional information on the art and science of creating happy success, you can find all this and more at our main site: **www.geniuscatalyst.com**.

Happy exploring!

ACKNOWLEDGMENTS

And now . . . have you ever seen one of those awards ceremonies where the winners try to list—in two minutes or less—every single person who has contributed to their success?

My heartfelt thanks and appreciation go to:

- Bill Cumming, Mandy Evans, Dr. Richard Bandler, and Paul McKenna, Ph.D.—I shudder to think what my life would have been like if you had not become a part of it!

- Alcinoo Giandinoto, Kerri Glass, and Jessica Abiva, who have kept my business (and life) moving forward whenever I needed to take a step back

- All the readers of the MNCT and members of the Genius Catalyst community who have supported me and my work during the past seven years

- Jane Acton, Sue Crowley, Dotti Irving, and Robert Kirby for their determination and persistence in getting my voice out into the world

- My wonderful editor, Lizzie Hutchins, who understands that a real argument isn't a dispute to be settled but a work of art to be evolved

- Jill Kramer, Lisa Mitchell, and Riann Bender for their adaptability and attention to detail

- The incredible staff at Hay House, in particular Michelle Pilley and Reid Tracy, whose unwavering belief in me is one of the most incredible gifts in my life

The people on this list are special and their contribution to this book has been tremendous. It includes the giants on whose practical and philosophical shoulders I stand, as well as the teachers, mentors, coaches, and friends who have supported me along the way.

Oli Barry	Sophie Keller
David Beeler	Nancy Kline
Steve Chandler	Tom Konkle
Michele Lisenbury Christensen	John LaValle
Larry Crane	Jennifer Louden
Dr. John F. Demartini	Robert Mintz, Ph.D.
Robert B. Dilts	Dr. James Pawelski
Bruce Di Marsico	Jay Perry
Ray Dodd	Candace B. Pert, Ph.D.
Hale Dwoskin	Lynn Robinson
Peter Fenner	Dr. Ronald A. Ruden
Gay and Kathlyn Hendricks	Dr. Martin Seligman
Byron Katie	Clare Staples
Barry Neil Kaufman	Win Wenger, Ph.D.

Finally, to my patient and supportive family, Nina, Oliver, Clara, and Maisy—I can come out and play now! May you always know how incredibly much you are loved.

ABOUT THE AUTHOR

Michael Neill, the best-selling author of *You Can Have What You Want,* is an internationally renowned success coach and a licensed master trainer of Neuro-Linguistic Programming (NLP). His weekly coaching column is syndicated in newspapers and magazines worldwide, and he's the host of *You Can Have What You Want* on **HayHouseRadio.com**®.

Website: **www.geniuscatalyst.com**

NOTES

NOTES

<u>NOTES</u>

NOTES

<u>NOTES</u>